Keeping American Schools Safe

Keeping American Schools Safe

A Handbook for Parents,
Students, Educators, Law Enforcement
Personnel and the Community

ANNE G. GARRETT

McFarland & Company, Inc., Publishers
Jefferson, North Carolina, and London

ISBN 0-7864-1147-3 (softcover binding : 50# alkaline paper) ∞

Library of Congress cataloguing data are available

British Library cataloguing data are available

Manufactured in the United States of America

Cover image © 2001 Art Today

*McFarland & Company, Inc., Publishers
Box 611, Jefferson, North Carolina 28640
www.mcfarlandpub.com*

To the children who
have been killed, injured
or traumatized by school violence.

If this book reaches one child or parent,
the author's goal has been accomplished.

Contents

Introduction

The headlines have been horrifying. The names of once obscure towns are now familiar, linked to nearly overwhelming tragedy: Littleton, Colorado; Jonesboro, Arkansas; West Paducah, Kentucky; Springfield, Oregon. In all, more than a dozen dead, two dozen injured, countless traumatized. Most horrifying of all, the accused gunmen are all children: the oldest 16, the youngest only 11. The mental, moral, and spiritual health of children around the country has become suspect.

Arguments rage over the possible causes of the rash of shootings—lack of family values, violent popular culture, the easy accessibility of guns. In the torrent of news and analysis that's resulted, clear-cut answers are difficult to find; even the extent of the problem of violent youth has been hard to determine. The important questions remain, however: what can parents, students, educators, law enforcement, and other community members do to prevent violence committed by and against our children?; and how can the risk of such violence be minimized in the future?

A child with a gun set the nation thinking about the unthinkable.

Two years after Barry Loukaitis killed three people in Moses Lake, Washington, a second child opened fire in Springfield, Oregon, in another year of violence across the nation.

Today, we are not much further along in ensuring our schools are safe.

Chapter One gives the grim statistics on school violence in our nation. It goes into great detail, as teachers, administrators, and students are polled and interviewed. The data collected paints a vivid portrait of the troubled youth in our country. A legal update is provided and includes court cases, general statutes and due process.

Chapter Two portrays characteristics of children with violent tendencies; actual profiles are included in this chapter. Facets of each profile are discussed in detail and a checklist is provided for assessing violent juvenile behavior.

Chapter Three focuses on school prevention and intervention. Effective programs from throughout the nation have been collected and are highlighted.

Chapter Four involves parents and what they can do to curb violence in our youth. Items include parenting skills meetings, volunteering, and getting help.

Chapter Five gives tips on how communities can work together to reduce crime rates while making our schools safer.

CHAPTER ONE

Violence in the Classrooms and Schools

A Manhattan six-year-old arrived at his elementary school one day with a loaded .25 caliber semiautomatic pistol tucked in his belt. He said he needed to have something for Show-and-Tell.

At DeKalb Junior-Senior School in Missouri, a student brought a .45 caliber automatic to school and fired five shots during his first period social studies class, killing a classmate. He then shot himself.

Violence in society is more evident now than ever before. Media and entertainment have opened up violent images for children to view. Easy availability of weapons to school-age children seems unreal and incredible. News stories of children bringing guns and weapons to school and killing classmates is disturbing, yet real. What is happening to our schools? What is happening to our classrooms? What is happening to our society and to our culture?

Two students and one teacher were killed and one other wounded when 14-year-old Barry Loukaitis opened fire in his algebra class (Moses Lake, Washington, 2-2-96). A principal and a student were killed and two wounded by Evan Ramsey, 16, at his high school in Bethel, Alaska (2-19-96).

An assistant principal was shot in the leg as he tried to wrestle a gun from the pocket of a 17-year-old student outside a crowded class-

3

room. A single shot rang out in the third floor hallway of John Bartram High School in southwest Philadelphia. The alleged gunman, armed with a .22 caliber handgun, fled but was arrested two blocks from the school by a police officer (10-4-96, Philadelphia).

Two students were killed and seven wounded by a 16 year old who was also accused of killing his mother. He and several friends were thought to be in a plot together; they wanted to be outcasts and worshipped Satan (10-1-97, Pearl, Mississippi).

Three students were killed and five wounded by a 14 year old as they participated in a prayer circle at Heath High School (West Paducah, Kentucky, 12-1-97).

Colt Todd, 14, was hiding in the woods when he shot and wounded two students as they stood in the parking lot of their school (Stamps, Arkansas, 12-15-97).

Four students and one teacher were killed, and ten others were wounded, outside Westside Middle School as it emptied during a false fire alarm. Mitchell Johnson, 13, and Andrew Golden, 11, shot their classmates and teachers from the woods (Jonesboro, Arkansas, 3-24-98).

A student was killed in the parking lot at Lincoln High School three days before he was to graduate. The victim was dating the ex-girlfriend of the killer, 18. One teacher was killed, and two students were wounded, at a dance at James W. Parker High School. A 14-year-old boy was charged (Edinboro, Pennsylvania, 4-24-98).

Two students were killed and 22 wounded in the cafeteria at Thurston High School by 15-year-old Kip Kinkel. Kinkel had been arrested and released in his parents' custody a day earlier, after it was discovered he had brought a gun to school. His parents were later found dead in their home (Springfield, Oregon, 5-21-98).

A 14-year-old boy in the hallway at Richmond High School, Richmond, Virginia, wounded one teacher and a guidance counselor (6-16-98).

Fourteen students and one teacher were killed, and 23 others were wounded, at Columbine High School in the nation's deadliest school shooting—Eric Harris, 18, and Dylan Klebold, 17, had plotted for a year to kill at least 500 and blow up their school. At the end of their hour-long rampage, they killed themselves (Littleton, Colorado, 5-20-99).

A 15-year-old boy who was reportedly depressed after breaking up with his girlfriend injured six students at Heritage High School (Conyers, Georgia, 5-20-99).

One student was killed and one wounded at W.R. Myers High School in the first fatal high school shooting in Canada in 20 years.

The suspect, a 14-year-old boy, had been unhappy and dropped out in order to begin home schooling (Taber, Alberta, Canada, 5-28-99).

These news headlines are reality. The serious fatalities and injuries happened in schools across the nation. This is a school official's and a parent's worst nightmare. How can one know who is capable of doing this? How can one prevent this from happening in our school and community? The experts agree on one thing—the random shootings that struck from Alaska to Virginia were unpredictable. There are preventive measures that can be taken, but prevention must begin at an early age to ingrain behavior patterns so students will learn how to handle conflict without resorting to violence.

"At a time when we are doing everything we can to strengthen our nation for the 21st Century, we cannot afford to let the threat of violence in our schools and our communities stand between our children and the education they need to make the most of their lives. We must take action to prevent youth violence before it happens" (President Bill Clinton, October 15, 1998).

President Clinton and First Lady Hillary Rodham Clinton hosted the White House Conference on School Safety (October 15, 1998), bringing together youth and violence experts and advocates, educators, elected officials, law enforcement and prevention and intervention practitioners, to discuss and learn more about what can be done to stop violence in America's schools. At the conference, the President discussed the findings from the First Annual Report on School Safety, prepared by the Departments of Justice and Education. The following information was shared:

- The overall crime rate in schools has dropped since 1993.
- Most schools are safer than the community at large.
- Students are more than twice as likely to experience serious violent crimes while out of school, and the worst violent victimizations occur in or near schools.
- Serious crimes and violence are concentrated in a small percentage of schools.
- Only about 10 percent of public schools report serious or violent crimes to the police.
- About 46 percent of schools report less serious or nonviolent crimes to police, and 43 percent of schools report no crime at all.
- Violence is more likely in larger, urban schools with older children.

- One-third of larger schools (more than 1,000 students) report serious violent crimes to the police, compared with less than one-tenth of small schools.
- Urban schools are twice as likely as rural schools to report serious violent crimes, and middle and high schools are four times more likely than elementary schools to report such crimes.
- Fistfights and theft are the most common school crimes. Overall, physical attacks and fights without weapons are the crimes most often reported to police by middle and high schools.
- Theft is the most common school crime.

The Center for the Prevention of School Violence has gathered information concerning the procedures which are being used across the United States to track school violence incidents. This review was prompted by President Clinton's call for the development of an Annual Report Card on school violence. Findings which reflect information from state departments of education or departments of criminal justice reveal that eight states are creating detailed reports of school crime or violence, and eight states are keeping track of such crime and violence in less-detailed reports. Thirty-four states do not have reporting systems except those required by the Gun-Free Schools Act of 1994.

The eight states which are creating detailed reports are Alabama, California, Delaware, Florida, North Carolina, Pennsylvania, South Carolina and Virginia. The crimes or incidents which are being reported in these states reflect common concerns about what threatens the safety and security of schools. Assertive behavior, various forms of inappropriate sexual conduct, and weapons violations are documented by all eight states. Drug incidents are reported in seven of the eight as are incidents which involve the victimization of school personnel.

Eight states (Georgia, Colorado, Idaho, Illinois, Indiana, Kansas, Maryland and Wisconsin) are creating much less detailed reports of incidents of discipline problems, suspensions, or expulsions. The level of detail varies among the states. Kansas uses a crime matrix which asks for a listing of felonies and misdemeanors which occur during a normal school day, on school property outside a normal school day, and on supervised activities outside a normal school day. Maryland asks for much more detail and presents it in the "Maryland Public School Suspension Form."

Overall, the collection and reporting of incidents occurring on school property illustrate that concerns exist about school crime and violence. The documenting of these incidents allows the authorities to better determine what is occurring and the frequency of occurrence.

Selected Research Findings on School Violence

The following research findings from 1997 and 1998 provide some understanding of what is happening in our schools today. They provide information reflective of different perspectives (students', teachers', principals'), different grade levels, and different concerns and problems.

Fifty-seven percent of public elementary and secondary school principals reported that one or more incidents of crime or violence occurred in their schools and were reported to law enforcement officials.

Ten percent of all public schools experienced one or more serious crimes (defined as murder, rape or other types of sexual battery, a physical attack or fight with a weapon, or robbery) during the school year that were reported to law enforcement.

Physical attacks or fights without a weapon led the list of reported crimes in public schools with about 190,000 such incidents reported.

Forty-five percent of grade schools reported one or more violent incidents compared with 74 percent of middle and 77 percent of high schools.

Some 6,093 students were expelled during the academic year for bringing firearms or explosives to schools.

Fifty-six percent of the students expelled for bringing firearms or explosives to school were high school students, 34 percent were junior high, and 9 percent were in elementary school.

The percentage of students reporting street gang presence at schools nearly doubled between 1989 and 1995, increasing from 15 percent to 28 percent.

An estimated 16 percent of all high school students in this country have been in one or more physical fights on school property in the course of a year.

Seventy-six percent of high school students and 46 percent of middle school students say drugs are kept or sold on school grounds.

Twenty-eight percent of high school and 19 percent of middle school teachers say students who appear drunk or high show up in their classes monthly or more frequently.

The percentage of elementary teachers who say students disrupt the classroom most of the time or fairly often has increased from 48 percent in 1984 to 65 percent in 1997.

The percentage of elementary teachers who say students talk back or disobey teachers most of the time or fairly often has increased from 42 percent in 1984 to 54 percent in 1997.

Forty-six percent of secondary school teachers said that disruptions often interfere with teaching and learning.

The most recent Youth Risk Behavior Survey found that 10 percent of high school students had carried a weapon (gun, knife, or club) on school property.

Fear of school-related violence kept 5 percent of high school students home at least once in the month prior to the most recent survey.

The extent of violence in our society is a cause for additional concern. Violence and violence-related injuries are particularly common among school age children. Therefore, when we speak of school violence, we are not referring to an isolated phenomenon relevant only to school settings. School violence is a true reflection of what is taking place in our communities.

During 1997, about 4,000 incidents of rape or other types of sexual battery were reported in our nation's public schools. There were about 11,000 incidents of physical attacks or fights in which weapons were used and 7,000 robberies in school that year.

"No matter where you are, parents want their students to be safe and secure ... that might even precede a quality education...." With drugs, gangs, and guns on the rise in many communities the threat of violence "weighs heavily on most principals' minds these days.... Anyone who thinks they are not vulnerable is heavily naïve" (Principal Michael Durso, Springbrook High School, as quoted in the *Washingtonian* Magazine, September 1997).

In inner-city communities, violence often is dramatically evident in night-time shootings and in the daytime struggle of families to keep their children from becoming perpetrators or victims. However, the problem of youth violence is not limited to urban environments. Domestic violence, hate crimes, sexual violence, and violence among peers pose threats to children and teenagers in every American community. No one is immune to the pervasive violence in American schools and society, but the probabilities of involvement are affected by race, social and economic class, age, geographical location, population density and other factors.

Violence is most prevalent among the poor, regardless of race. At a time when most immigrants were poor whites, rates of violence among them also were very high. Fifteen percent of children growing up in nonminority homes are poor, but 38 percent and up to 90 percent of Native American children grow up in poverty. Few differences among the races are found in rates of violence when people at the same economic level or income level are compared.

To be poor in America is to be segregated, often in inner cities, in which crime and the threat of crime confine the poor to fear and isolation at best and death at worst. Violence rates in central cities are 41.3 per thousand; but in the suburbs and nonmetropolitan areas they are 25.2 per thousand. In comparison to nonminorities, higher proportions of ethnic minority populations live in cities.

The widespread ownership of firearms in the United States has persisted throughout American history and is unique among western industrialized nations. Between 40 percent and 50 percent of American households have guns, half of which are handguns. According to the National Rifle Association, approximately 200 million firearms are in households. Students carry an estimated 270,000 guns to school each day.

The alarming rise in youth homicide is related to the availability of firearms. Between 1979 and 1989, there was a 61 percent increase in homicides by shootings committed by 15-to 19-year-old white and African-American youth. During the same period, the rate of homicides by objects other than guns declined 29 percent. According to the U.S. Centers for Disease Control and Prevention, firearms accounted for about three-fourths of the killings by African-American youth.

Some youths say they carry a gun because they are afraid of the others who have guns. Male teenagers who have dropped out of high school are three times more likely to say they own one or more handguns than those still in school. In a study of 11th grade students in Washington high schools, 6 percent reported owning handguns and admitted to having been expelled or suspended from school, having sold guns, or having engaged in assault and battery.

Easy access to guns by violence-prone people is related to homicide rates. The greater the number and availability of guns, the greater the chances that these weapons will be used by a relatively few violence-prone adolescents. This does not necessarily mean, however, that there will be larger numbers of adolescents using guns.

Youth can easily obtain firearms, and they see them frequently in films and on television as a method of solving problems. Nonetheless, few violence-prevention programs for youth focus specifically on preventing violence with guns. The school's resources are devoted to disarming students who are carrying guns. The widespread access to firearms necessitates more education for children and adults on how to avoid or prevent firearm violence.

The use of alcohol and drugs is related to violence in our schools. Alcohol seems to lower inhibition toward violent behavior. Youth who are involved in drug trafficking have a greater risk of being involved in violence. Substance-abusing parents are more apt to become physically abusive, sexually abusive, or neglectful in ways that expose children to risk of abuse by others.

Only a small percentage of youth join delinquent gangs and the amount of violence by gang members is small. However, homicide and aggravated assault are three times more likely to be committed by gang members than by nongang delinquents. The new roles for younger and older gang members reflect the increase of gang involvement in drugs. Male gang members outnumber females by 20 to 1, and females commit less than 5 percent of gang crime.

Teens are 2½ times more likely to be victims of violent crimes than those over the age of 20, and much of this violence occurs at school. In some communities, violence is part of daily life. In a study of eighth graders in Chicago, 73 percent had seen someone stabbed, shot, robbed or killed.

The statistics on school violence are staggering. Consider: About 10 percent of school children ages 10 to 19 admit they have fired a gun at someone or have been fired upon. About three million crimes occur on or near school each year, and half of all violent crimes against teenagers occur on or near schools. More than 80 percent of over 2,000 school districts responding to a 1993 National School Boards Association survey, believe school violence is currently worse than it was five years ago. As early as 1984, the U.S. Surgeon General legitimized violence as a public health issue, and in the 1990s the nation's governors and Congress declared in the National Educational Goals that safe schools are essential to effective schools.

The Safe School Study found that teenagers were at greater risk of becoming victims of violence while at school than when away from school. Although teenage youth spend 25 percent of their day in school, 40 percent of robberies and 36 percent of the assaults on urban teenagers occurred at school (U.S. Department of Health, Education and Welfare).

In high schools 5,200 teachers, or .5 percent of all high school teachers, were attacked physically each month. The attacks on teachers were five times more likely to result in serious injury than attacks on students. The study determined that about 80 percent of personal violence took place during school time. The classroom was the safest place in school for students; students were found to be in the greatest risk when they were in the hallways or between classes.

The risk of personal violence also increased with the size of the community. It was more prevalent in high schools than in elementary schools, and greatest at the junior high or middle school level. For students aged 12 to 15, 68 percent of robberies and 50 percent of assaults occurred at school.

California provides the best source of current information for violence in the schools. Since the 1985–86 school year, the state has required all schools to keep statistics on crime. The numbers collected during the first four years contained good news—theft, substance abuse, felony sex and offenses declined. But, assaults against students and staff increased. Also, the category of assault/attack/menace increased by 16 percent (California Department of Public Education, 1990).

During the same four-year period, incidents of weapons possession rose 28 percent, with a 100 percent increase in the number of gun-related incidents: a 50 percent increase in elementary schools, a 79 percent increase in middle schools, and a staggering 142 percent increase at the high school level.

California was not the only state that witnessed an increase in violence in the schools. Florida experienced a 42 percent increase in gun incidents during the 1987–88 school year (Center to Prevent Handgun Violence).

For many years, North Carolina has led the nation in pursuing efforts directed at reducing youth violence and making schools safer. The state's efforts intensified when Governor Jim Hunt charged the Task Force on School Violence to find solutions to school violence. As a result of the implementation of several recommendations, North Carolina schools have become safer places for students and teachers. Since 1993-94, the rate of reported incidents of school violence has declined 19 percent and the number of guns brought to school has dropped 65 percent. Youth violence has also been addressed, with juvenile justice reform now being implemented and the number of juveniles arrested for murder down 28 percent since 1995.

The Center to Prevent Handgun Violence reports nationwide, during the four academic years beginning September 1986, at least 75 people were killed with guns at school, 201 were severely wounded, and 242 were held hostage by gun-wielding assailants.

Why are weapons, particularly guns, finding their way into the schools? For every United States household, there are two guns in the hands of private citizens. Sadly enough, these guns are finding their way into our children's hands. In crime-laden areas, students often carry weapons for protection against muggers, drug-users who rob to support their habits, and attacks by gang members.

Even adults in schools are not immune to carrying weapons. Three San Francisco high school teachers admitted to reporters that they carry weapons. "One even displayed the razor-sharp blade he keeps in his jacket for self-defense. The teacher said, 'The kids have knives. They have guns in their lockers. What's to stop them from using them?'" (Butterfield and Turner, 1989).

The report entitled "Violence and Discipline Problems in U.S. Public Schools: 1996-1997" constitutes the first of five reports on discipline and violence to be released during the upcoming years. The report was designed to collect data and to examine the frequency of violent incidents in elementary and secondary schools. Questionnaires were sent to 1,234 regular public elementary, middle and high schools. The survey indicated that only 10 percent of schools experienced one or more serious crimes such as murder, rape or sexual battery, suicide, robbery, physical attacks or crimes with weapons. Forty-three percent of the schools reported no incidents of crime, and 37 percent reported from one to five crimes. In schools that experienced crime, the less serious violent crimes were more prevalent, such as physical attacks or fights without a weapon, theft, larceny and vandalism.

The survey results demonstrate that the number of crimes experienced by schools is related to certain school characteristics. Elementary schools reported fewer incidents of serious crime than middle and high schools. The difference between the number of incidents of robbery in elementary and middle schools was less significant.

Smaller schools were less likely to report serious violent crimes than medium-sized and larger schools. Incidents of serious crimes were more prevalent in city schools than schools in towns, but did not differ significantly between city and rural or urban fringe schools. Schools with greater percentages of minority enrollment were more likely to experience serious violent crimes.

Principals were asked to report the extent to which specific discipline issues were a problem in their schools during the 1996-1997 school year so that a relationship between discipline and crime could be examined.

Areas for the ratings included:

- Student tardiness.
- Student absenteeism.
- Physical conflicts among students.
- Robbery or theft of items worth $10.00.
- Vandalism of school property.
- School alcohol use.
- Student drug use.
- Sale of drugs on school grounds.
- Student tobacco use.
- Possession of weapons.
- Trespassing.
- Verbal abuse of teachers.
- Physical abuse of teachers.
- Teacher absenteeism.
- Teacher alcohol or drug use.
- Racial tensions and gangs.

The principals perceived these discipline issues in their schools as no more than minor problems (43 percent) or moderate problems (41 percent). Sixteen percent of public principals perceived at least one discipline issue as a serious problem.

The discipline issues most cited during the 1996-97 school year included: tardiness—40 percent; absenteeism or cutting classes—25 percent; physical conflicts—21 percent. Principals indicated through the survey that teacher alcohol or drug use, physical abuse of teachers, sale of drugs on school grounds, and student possession of weapons were serious or moderate problems at their schools.

Principals were more likely to perceive a discipline issue as a serious problem in high schools and schools with enrollments of more than 1,000 students. Principals with the lowest serious discipline problems were those in elementary schools, then those in middle schools. Twice as many principals in high schools reported serious discipline problems (37 percent). Thirty-eight percent of principals in large schools reported some serious discipline problems compared with 15 percent of principals in medium-sized schools and 10 percent of principals in small schools.

Discipline issues most frequently reported as moderate differed by instructional level, school size, and location of school, minority enrollment, and percentage of students on free or reduced lunches. For elementary and high schools, student tardiness and student absenteeism or class cutting were among the three most often cited offenses (32 and

67 percent respectively). Principals of elementary and middle schools also reported physical conflicts among students as one of their top three serious or moderate discipline problems (18 percent and 35 percent respectively). In the high schools, student tobacco, drug and alcohol use were more often reported as serious or moderate problems than physical conflicts among students (48, 36, and 27 percent respectively compared with 17 percent).

Hal Burbach with the Curry School of Education completed a study, "Violence and the Public Schools," citing the following facts:

- African-American males, ages 15–19, are ten times more likely to be murdered than white males.
- African-American females are nearly five times more likely to be murdered than white females.
- The portion of America's youth arrested for violent crimes rose from only three-tenths of 1 percent in 1982 to five-tenths of 1 percent in 1992.
- Criminologists expect juvenile crime to rise by 114 percent over the next decade.
- It costs $39,000 per year to keep a youth in a correctional center.
- The average child witnesses depictions of 8,000 murders and 100,000 other acts of violence before finishing elementary school.

Characteristics of Serious or Chronic Juvenile Offenders
- Delinquency case before age 13.
- Low income family.
- Child deemed troublesome by teachers and peers at age eight to ten.
- Poor school performance by age ten.
- Psychomotor clumsiness.
- Low nonverbal I.Q.
- Sibling convicted of crime.
- Head injury and/or physical/sexual abuse.

How the Public Feels About Crime
Forty-three percent say there's more crime in their neighborhoods than a year ago; 17 percent say less.

Sixty-four percent want stiffer gun laws.

While many Americans believe that juveniles cause most of the crime, the actual amount they do is 12.8 percent.

The 1993 Gallup Poll shows 80 percent favor putting more police on the streets—and paying higher taxes to do it.

Eighty-two percent want to make it harder to parole violent inmates.

Seventy-nine percent want tougher sentences for all crimes.

Possible Cause of Violence

- We're a violent species.
- We're a violent nation.
- The role of the media.

Is there a connection between the break-up of the American family and the increase of gangs? Disorderly conduct can be distinguished by childhood onset (about 4 percent) and adolescent onset (about 96 percent). The childhood onset group commits over 50 percent of the crimes in their age group, and they tend to be more violent crimes.

Contributors to Violence

Prenatal substance abuse, assaults, neglect, low birth weight, head injury, undetected disease.

Bonding trust deficits, media violence, violent role models, lack of alternative activities, dim view of education/job.

Inadequate housing/income, machismo/saving face, discrimination, lack of social skills, allure of money.

Deviance, gangs and guns.

If You Have a Gun at Home

You are eight times more likely to be killed by or to kill a family member or intimate acquaintance.

You are three times more likely to be killed by or kill someone in your home.

You or a family member are 5 times more likely to commit suicide.

Violence in the Home

Ball State researchers surveyed 3,357 high school students and found that 74 percent sanctioned hitting a sibling after being hit first.

Nearly 10 percent sanctioned hitting a wife when she would not listen to reason.

Percent of Principals Reporting Incidents (1993)

Incident	Suburban	Urban
Girls fighting	59 percent	41 percent

Boys fighting	43 percent	34 percent
Gang-related	43 percent	31 percent
Gun-related	38 percent	26 percent
Drug-related	26 percent	17 percent
Fights/different races	20 percent	23 percent

The rates of young people being assaulted at school is the same today as it was in 1976. In fact, there were 27 percent fewer in the 1997-98 school year than in 1992-93.

Juvenile crime, which began climbing in 1987, actually has fallen in the past two years, and juvenile homicides have declined 30 percent since 1994.

In 1997, 8.5 percent of high school students reported carrying a weapon to school at least once in the month prior to being surveyed. Overall, male students (12.5 percent) were significantly more likely than female students (3.7 percent) to have brought a weapon to school. One study reported more than 6,000 students were expelled for taking firearms to school during the 1996-97 year. Of those, 56 percent were in high school, 34 percent in junior high school and 9 percent in elementary school. In 1997, 7.4 percent of high school students were threatened or injured with a weapon on school property at least once.

Effects of Crime and Violence and School Attendance

In 1997, 4 percent of high school students reported missing school during the prior month because they felt unsafe either at school or when traveling to and from school.

Latino (7.2 percent) and black (6.8 percent) students were significantly more likely than white (2.4 percent) students to have felt unsafe. More ninth grade female (5.8 percent) and male (5.2 percent) students missed school for this reason than did 12th grade female (3 percent) and male (2.3 percent).

Most public schools report having a zero tolerance policy toward serious student offenses such as violence and use of tobacco, alcohol, drugs and weapons. Zero tolerance policies are those where schools or districts have mandated predetermined consequences for various student offenses. The percentage of schools having these policies range from 79 to 94.

Most schools employ low levels of security measures to prevent violence. Only 2 percent of public schools have stringent security (a full-time guard and daily or random metal detector checks). Eleven percent of schools have instituted moderate security measures such as full-time guards, while 84 percent of public schools have a low level of security and restricted access to their schools but no guards or metal detectors.

Factors contributing to school violence are numerous, complex, and mostly community related. Teachers perceive that the major factors contributing to student violence are lack of parental supervision at home (71 percent), lack of family involvement with the school (66 percent) and exposure to violence in the mass media (55 percent) (*The American Teacher*, 1993). Teachers also believe that certain types of parenting produce children who contribute to school violence.

America's children are exposed to a steady stream of verbal and physical violence that begins early and continues throughout their lives. Numerous reports have cited the fact that children in the United States spend more time watching television than they do attending school. Most of the things children watch, including cartoons, is unsupervised and much of it is filled with unadulterated sex and violence.

Our children today have unlimited access to the Internet and the many chat rooms and search engines that are available. Recently a student in Waynesville, North Carolina, made a tennis ball bomb; he got the recipe and instructions from the Internet. The Internet is like fire—a wonder and a danger, with ability to enhance lives dramatically or destroy them. Reams of valuable information are available at the touch of a keyboard. So are pornographers, instructions for making bombs and guns, and sexual predators who will lure children through chat rooms or e-mail.

Thirty-six percent of students concur that lack of parental supervision at home is the major factor contributing to violence in schools. However, 34 percent of them cite as a second factor the presence of gang or group membership or peer pressure (*The American Teacher*, 1993). Several studies concluded that peer group pressure is perhaps the fastest growing and most distributing cause of acts of violence among youths, whether in school or out (*The American Teacher*, 1993).

The United States Department of Justice conducted a study in 1991 and they concluded that students cited drugs and alcohol as the third most potent factor in school violence. Those who reported the availability of drugs in school did not vary significantly by ethnicity, level of family income, or geographical location. The reports indicate that the use of heroin, cocaine, marijuana, and crack is down among students in grades five to 12, but the consumption of alcohol is not. Alcohol is the number one drug used by teenagers and young adults.

Another factor in school violence is the emerging trend of acts related to race or religion. "The 1993 Lou Harris Study on Racism and

Violence in American High Schools: Project Teamwork Responds," reports that racism and violence are rising in America's high schools. Seventy-five percent of all students surveyed reported seeing or hearing about racially or religiously motivated confrontations on a regular basis, up from the 57 percent in an earlier study.

Most teachers believe that violence occurs in hallways or under staircases, in the cafeteria, in the parking lot, or in unsupervised classrooms. Students concur that most acts of violence occur in these places, but add the gym and locker rooms as prime sites. Students are also victimized in restrooms. Most acts of violence occur where adult supervision is minimal or where large numbers of people assemble.

Victims of violence in the schools cover a wide range. Over 900 teachers are threatened, and over 2,000 students and nearly 40 teachers are physically attacked on school grounds every hour of each school day each year, according to Keith Geiger, President of the National Education Association. The Department of Justice states that every day in the United States, 100,000 students carry guns to school and 40 students are injured or killed by guns (U.S. Department of Education and Justice).

Younger children, grades six to ten, are more likely to be victims of violence in our schools than senior high school students. The Department of Justice reported that students whose families moved frequently and students from racial or ethnic groups that are minorities within the school are more likely to be physically assaulted. Students who wear expensive clothing or jewelry, or who bring video equipment, cassette players, beepers and other electronic devices to school, are more likely to be victims of property crime.

Teachers are also victims of violence in the school setting. Although the majority of teachers believe they are unlikely victims of violence in and around school, the opposite is true. Most teachers feel safe in their schools during the day, but after school hours many teachers, especially those in urban areas, do not. Women and younger, less experienced teachers are targets, but they are not the primary victims of violence among staff members. Teachers who are considered to be strict, and who insist that students adhere to rigorous academic and behavior standards are most at risk of being victimized. Thirty-eight percent of teachers and 57 percent of students rank strict teachers as more at risk of victimization than any other members of the school staff. This perception could have a dramatic effect on school districts that are attempting to strengthen accountability standards.

Basically, any administrator can affirm that there are three groups of students in a school, who fit into what they call the 80-15-5 rule. Eighty percent of the students rarely break the rules of the school. Fifteen percent break the rules on a regular basis by refusing to accept classroom principles and restrictions. If not clearly apprised of expectations and consequences of such behavior, these students can disrupt learning for all other students. The last five percent of the students are chronic rule breakers and are generally out of control most of the time. They may commit acts of violence in the school and the community. Other school administrators adhere to the 90-10 rule, which means they spend ninety percent of their time taking care of ten percent of their school population.

Thus, the public's concern about discipline and violence in our schools is valid. Violence caused by school-age children (in and out of school) is worse now than ever before; it is on the rise and permeates every segment of American society. This is not to say, however, that all of today's youth present discipline problems or are perpetrators of acts of violence: that would be oversimplifying the issue. On the contrary, the vast majority of our youth are not violent, nor have they committed acts of violence.

A recent survey conducted on behalf of a group of news outlets across Washington State by Mason-Dixon Political Media Research, Inc., of Columbia, Maryland, indicated that Washington residents think guns, drugs, and violence have made their schools more dangerous in the last ten years. The telephone survey contacted 828 adults in Washington. The respondents were randomly selected throughout the state based on population patterns. Two-thirds of all people contacted said they thought schools were less safe in the last ten years. Fifty-five percent of the women surveyed said they were concerned about the safety of their children in the local school district. However, fewer than one in three men were very concerned about local school safety. Women also were more concerned that weapons pose a very serious problem for school safety. Two other areas of concern listed as very serious were drugs and violence.

Those surveyed said parents should be held responsible for safety in the local schools. About two-thirds said parents were very responsible for making sure their schools are safe and free of violence. Fifty percent said school staff are very responsible, and only a third thought students were responsible.

The survey respondents felt that adding additional counselors at the school would be helpful instead of metal detectors, surveillance cameras, security officers, or even smaller class size. Three out of every five respondents felt that counselors should be added to every elementary school to identify and help troubled students at an early age.

Fifty percent thought smaller class sizes would be an effective remedy, but only one-third supported purchasing metal detectors.

Just how good are our public schools today? If one asks school teachers, the picture is bright. In fact, only 16 percent more gave an A or a B to their local public schools than do members of the general public, according to the Fourth Phi Delta Kappa Poll of Teachers' Attitudes Toward the Public School. Teachers' perceptions of how often their students misbehave in the classroom have changed since 1984. Fewer teachers today say they frequently find their students are truant or absent, vandalize or steal school property, skip class, drink alcohol, or have sex at school. Seventeen percent of the elementary teachers think that children frequently disrupt the classroom more than in 1984, and 12 percent more say that children are often disobedient. Ten percent more high school teachers than in 1984 believe their students frequently dress inappropriately or use drugs at school.

Teachers say that parents are less likely to support them if their child is disrupting the classroom than if they tell the parents their child is not working hard at school. More high school teachers (63 percent) than elementary teachers (48 percent) say parents would support them if their child was not working hard. Teachers' expectations of how much support they will get from parents fall short of what parents themselves say they would do.

Teachers were asked to estimate how frequently each of the following discipline problems occurred in their classrooms: homework not completed; behavior that disrupts class; talking back to the teacher; truancy/absenteeism; inappropriate dress; cheating; stealing; vandalizing; skipping class; using drugs; theft of school property; selling drugs at school; racial fights; carrying knives, firearms or other weapons; drinking alcoholic beverages at school; sexual activity at school; taking money by force; physical attacks on teachers or staff.

The percentage of teachers who say students misbehave either often or most of the time has dropped since 1984 for six discipline problems: truancy and absence, vandalism of school property, skipping classes, theft of school property, drinking alcohol at school, and sexual activity at school. The percentage has dropped since 1989 for five other problems: incomplete homework, sloppy dress, cheating, stealing personal property, and selling drugs at school.

The percentage of elementary teachers who say students disrupt the classroom and talk back to or disobey them most of the time has increased since 1984. The percentage of high school teachers who estimate the students dress inappropriately or use drugs at school most of the time has increased since 1984. Teachers' perception of the frequency of the two lowest-ranked problems—taking money or property by force/using weapons or threats, and physical attacks on teachers or staff—have remained stable.

With the exceptions of cheating on tests and sloppy or inappropriate dress, a greater percentage of inner-city teachers than teachers in other settings experience all discipline problems most of the time. A greater percentage of teachers in inner cities (65 percent) and urban areas (47 percent) than teachers in small towns (38 percent) and suburban areas (31 percent) estimate students are truant or absent most of the time. More teachers in the South (77 percent) than in the Midwest (48 percent), East (45 percent), or West (41 percent) say students talk back to and disobey them most of the time.

Legal Rights Against Violence

Schools have the right to take precautions to ensure safety. However, parents and students have a legal right regarding searches, seizures of property and disciplinary actions. School tragedies have underscored the need for policies, procedures and practices that are legally sound and defensible in preventing and confronting violence in the school.

While a major legal concern has been the infringement of rights protected by our Constitution, the United States Supreme Court held in a number of major decisions that the legitimate interest of the school in protecting others from violence or harm will outweigh any individual's right of expression.

In *Tinker* (1969), the court noted that when student speech hinders the ability of others to be secure and to be left alone, the limited First Amendment rights of a student must give way to the needs of the school. More difficult cases in the area of dress codes arise when the school administrator uses a dress-related rule to control political expression of students. In *Tinker v. Des Moines Independence School District,* three students were suspended from school when they violated a school policy by wearing black armbands to protest the Vietnam War. The Supreme Court found that school officials had punished the students for a silent, passive expression of opinion, unaccompanied by any disturbance or disorder, and thereby violated their free speech rights. The court concluded that a school system could not justify infringing students' First Amendment rights unless it could reasonably forecast substantial disruption of or material interference with school activities.

Two United States Supreme Court cases decided in the 1980s have modified the holding in *Tinker* and have been interpreted by lower courts to apply to student dress issues. In *Hazelwood School District No. 403 v. Kuhlmeier* (1988), the Supreme Court held that school officials may regulate or censor a student newspaper published as part of a journalism class. Following this decision, school officials were able to impose reasonable regulations on student speech in the context of school-sponsored expressive activities.

In *School District No. 403 v. Fraser* (1986), the United States Supreme Court acknowledged that in drafting student conduct codes, school officials cannot possibly anticipate all misconduct.

Student codes of conduct have been challenged as violating substantive due process in several contexts. Students have argued that a specific term in a code does not apply to their alleged misconduct. In 1982, a student argued that the rule he had been charged with violating did not apply to him because it was directed at students under the influence of drugs on the school premises, whereas he had been under the influence of alcohol. The United States Supreme Court concluded that alcohol was included within the definition of a drug and upheld the student's suspension. An Arkansas student argued that she should not be expelled under a students' conduct rule against the use or possession of intoxicating beverages; she admitted to having spiked the punch that was served at an extracurricular event for students and parents but argued that the small amount of beer she added did not make the punch an intoxicating beverage. The Supreme Court found that if the board interpreted the code as requiring disciplinary action when a student used or possessed beverages containing alcohol, which the punch certainly did, then the code provision could be applied to the student. In both of the foregoing cases, the Supreme Court deferred to the school board's interpretation of its own rules.

In *Hazelwood*, the court noted that a school need not tolerate student speech that is inconsistent with the basic educational mission of the school.

Students are entitled to be free from unreasonable searches just the same as adults outside the school are entitled. Nonetheless, the courts have given deference to the special roles that schools play in educating youth.

Washington school districts can grant students broader rights, but they can't be more restrictive than the state codes. Private schools don't have to abide with the same requirements as public schools.

In most states, school officials can search a student without a warrant. A search can be launched without any hard evidence of a crime, but reasonable suspicion must be present that a student has done something questionable. School officials must have a good reason to search luggage or bookbags before a field trip. If it is believed that a school policy or procedure has been broken then lockers and handbags may be searched. However, officials can't conduct strip searches that expose undergarments. School desks and lockers are school property so schools may check or search them as often as desired.

School districts are required to adopt written rules describing the type of misconduct for which students may be disciplined and make them available for parents and students. In many states these are called a Student Code of Conduct. It is also recommended that a due process or grievance procedure be available for students and parents. The majority of Student Codes of Conduct have these items included in them.

In emergency situations, a superintendent may expel students. The parent or guardian must be notified within 24 hours; this procedure is normally concluded by registered mail. Parents are then given 48 hours or five calendar days to apply for due process. Upon receiving the request the superintendent must respond in writing, giving the reasons for the disciplinary action. Parents may then request an appeal hearing. Normally, someone is designated in each school district to arrange these meetings.

When police officials are asked to interview students they must follow all the rules that protect adults. Students must have their Miranda Rights read to them, including the right to remain silent and the right to an attorney. Students under the age of 12 are unable to waive their rights without the consent of their parents or guardians.

The Fifth Amendment to the United States Constitution provides that no person shall be compelled in any criminal case to be a witness against himself. Neither an accused person nor a witness may be forced to testify against their own interests. In addition, in the landmark case *Miranda v. Arizona* (1966), the Supreme Court interpreted the Fifth Amendment to mean that before law enforcement officers may question a person they hold in custody, they must inform the person that they have the right to remain silent and that anything they say can be used against them.

In North Carolina, House Bill 517 was enacted due to the increase in bomb threats. House Bill 517 is an act which raises the criminal penalty for a second or subsequent offense of making a bomb threat or perpetrating a hoax by placing a false bomb at a public building, for bringing a bomb onto school property, and for the actual detonation of a bomb. It also provides for restitution of consequential damages resulting from bomb threats or hoaxes.

North Carolina requires each school and district to develop a Safe School Plan. Each plan has to be both local and state approved. One hundred percent of North Carolina schools have these plans and they establish a way to prevent and respond to violence. Each principal's incentive pay is based on the successful completion and documentation of a safe school.

A school district is not liable for the death of a student shot by another student in an off-campus altercation (*Hill v. Safford Unified School District*, 1997). The mother brought charges against the school district and the teacher for negligence and wrongful death because the student was involved in a verbal confrontation with a gang member while at school. The two students were taken to the office to defuse the situation and then they returned to class. After school that day, a crowd gathered because of the anticipation of a fight between the two boys. A teacher told them to take it elsewhere and called the police. The students then moved to an area outside town. There, the gang member shot the other student, and the police arrived shortly after the shooting. The court found that it was not foreseeable that the students would continue the fight elsewhere, despite the suggestion of the teacher. The court also noted that no school official was aware of the student bringing a gun on campus; therefore there was no evidence that the gang member was dangerous or a threat to others.

In *Brum v. Town of Dartmouth*, 1995, a violent altercation between two groups of youths resulted in the murder of a student on school property. The student's parent filed an action against the school district, the town and the municipal officials, alleging various civil rights violations and negligence. According to the complaint, school officials were aware of the tension between the two groups and had detained two students. Three youths entered the school building, armed with various weapons, and went in search of a student. Instead of locating the student they were looking for, the youths found and stabbed another student as he sat in his social studies class. The complaint alleged that the defendants failed to adopt and implement appropriate security policies and procedures as mandated by state law. The front door of the building, through which the youths entered, remained unlocked, and school officials failed to intervene after witnessing the alleged perpetrators entering the school building. This case went to superior court, and was appealed. In conclusion, the defendants may have prevented the attack and their failure to do so fell within the liability exception to the state tort claims act.

In *Morse v. Lower Merion School District* (1997), a school district was not liable for the death of a teacher shot by a local resident who had entered the school building through an unlocked back entrance, according to the 3rd United States Circuit Court of Appeals. The court ruled that trespassing and shooting were unforeseeable because the door had been left unlocked for school construction workers, and the shooter was considered mentally unstable. The teacher was shot and killed in her classroom before her students. The shooter was a local resident with a history of mental illness and was convicted of murder and incarcerated in a psychiatric hospital. The teacher's husband filed an action against the school district and the day care association that owned the center. The lawsuit alleged that the district had a written policy that all side and back entrances to the school were to be kept locked at all times. Additionally, although the school district was aware that the back door was left unlocked, it made no attempt to correct the condition. A district court dismissed the case finding that the school district did not create a particular danger to the teacher by leaving the back door open.

In *Wood v. Henry County Public Schools* (1998), the Virginia Supreme Court held that suspension and expulsion had not violated a student's due process rights. The parents and student were given notice of the charge and opportunity to present any information they deemed appropriate. The court rejected the student's argument that the school district should not be permitted to promulgate policies that require the suspension or expulsion of students who possess knives on school property. The student did not identify any statutory or constitutional rights violated by the school district.

Georgia's *Caldwell v. Griffin Spalding County Board of Education* (1998) held that school officials could not be held liable for failing to prevent a physical attack on a freshman football player. There was no evidence the defendants acted with malice or intent to cause injury. The court rejected the argument that a criminal statute against hazing subjected the defendants to liability for the student's injuries.

G.S. 115C–391(d2) in North Carolina provides that students who assault teachers or any other students may be subject to long-term suspension or removal to alternative education settings. This subsection specifies that if a student who is at least 13 years old physically assaults and seriously injures a teacher or other school personnel, the superintendent shall, upon recommendation of the principal, remove that student to an alternative educational setting. If the conduct leading to the removal occurs on or before the 90th school day, the board shall remove the student to the setting for the remainder of the school year and the first 90 school days in the following school year. If the conduct leading to the removal occurs after the 90th day, the board shall remove the student to that setting for the remainder of the school year and the entire subsequent school year.

If no appropriate alternative educational setting is available, the superintendent shall, upon recommendation of the principal, suspend any student who is at least 13 and physically assaults and seriously injures a teacher or other school employee for no less than 300 days, but no more than 365 days. The assault must have occurred on school premises or at a school function.

A weapon is any gun, rifle, pistol, or other firearm of any dynamite cartridge, bomb, grenade, mine or powerful explosive. School officials should note that the 365-day suspension is mandated for a student who brings a firearm to school. Thus a student who is found to possess a firearm on campus, but who did not bring it on campus is not subject to the 365-day suspension.

Givens v. Poe (1972), a North Carolina federal district case, listed the procedural safeguards that a student faced with a long-term suspension must receive. In the school system where Givens resided, only four students had ever had a hearing before a school board, and those hearings had not been held until more than 25 days after the original suspension. The court observed that suspensions without hearings had been the school system's "disciplinary weapon of choice." The court ordered the school system to implement procedures that would guarantee that the state's power over the students in public schools would be exercised with the due process of law. It held that a student faced with a suspension for a substantial period of time must be given procedural safeguards. The safeguards include:

1. Notice to parents and the student in the form of a written and specific statement to justify the punishment.
2. A full hearing after adequate notice (normally 48 hours or 5 calendar days).
3. An impartial tribunal.
4. The right to examine evidence against the student.
5. The right to be represented by counsel (not at public expense).
6. The right to confront and examine adverse witnesses.
7. The right to present evidence on behalf of the student.
8. The right to record the proceedings.
9. The requirement that the authorities' decision be based on substantial evidence.

There have not been any cases involving long-term suspension to reach the United States Supreme Court. *Givens v. Poe* serves as the guide for due process and students facing suspension for more than ten days. A student suspended for more than ten days may appeal the superintendent's decision to the school board. If the student wishes to appeal the board's decision, they may file a petition seeking review of the decision in the superior court of the county where the decision was made. This petition must be filed within 30 days of the board's decision.

Students also may file a lawsuit in either state or federal court if they believe school officials have violated their constitutional rights.

Local boards of education, upon the recommendation of the principal and superintendent, may expel any student who is 14 years old or older, and whose behavior indicates that the student's continued presence in the school constitutes a clear threat to the safety of students or employees.

Local boards of education must base their decision to expel on clear and convincing evidence. A student facing expulsion is threatened with the loss of their right to public education. Thus, before being deprived of this right, the student is entitled to a full administrative hearing before the local board of education with all the same components of a hearing provided for students facing a long-term suspension. Before ordering the expulsion of a student the local board of education must consider whether any alternative program offered by the local school system unit might provide educational services for the student.

Student conduct codes generally include a prohibition against assault and battery. An assault is an overt act, or an attempt, to injure another person physically. The most common form of assault is attempting to strike another person, but shoving, scratching, biting, pulling a chair out from under another, and throwing items are all forms of assault. Battery is the actual striking of another person. Under North Carolina law, a person who is convicted of a simple assault is guilty of a Class 1 misdemeanor.

The punishment for assaulting school personnel is stricter than simple assault. The penalty for assaulting an officer or employee of the State or any political subdivision of the State, when the officer is discharging their official duties or for assaulting a school bus driver, school bus monitor, or school employee who is boarding the school bus, or who is on the school bus, is a Class A1 misdemeanor. It is a general misdemeanor to assault a sports official while the official is performing official duties or immediately after the sports event at which the official worked.

Violence in the schools has never merited more concern than it does today. Although some types of school crime have decreased in recent years, violence seems to be spreading and intensifying—not only in the schools, but in American communities large and small. Educators, criminologists and law enforcement personnel have worked to create effective methods to control current school violence and to prevent such violence in the future.

Schools are an integral part of society. As behaviors change, in society as a whole and in individual communities, those changes are reflected in the school. We live in a society in which police battle the rising tide of drug traffickers, drive-by gang shootings punctuate weekends, and half of the households in the nation possess firearms. We shouldn't be surprised that violence has reached the classroom and the school. Violence in the schools shocks and horrifies us. We want our children to be safe from harm—at school and at home.

Since the 1960s, crime and violence have been increasing in schools. As public concern about violence grew, educators and legislators took new initiatives to tighten up school security. Educators, parents and community members are striving to determine the causes of violence and attempting to develop strategies to control and prevent it.

In Lansing, Michigan, a 16-year-old boy shot a social studies teacher in the chest in the hallway outside the teacher's classroom. The boy was angry because he had been thrown off the soccer team.

A physical education teacher was beaten unconscious by an intruder after he surprised the man rifling through students' gym bags outside a Bronx school. During a shop class supervised by a substitute teacher, a Florida middle school student was trapped by two other boys in an area screened by a chalkboard at the back of the room. The boy was struck and threatened, then forced to perform oral sex on one of the tormentors while several other students watched out for teachers. The victim was an emotionally handicapped student who had been mainstreamed.

Incidents like these devastate the lives of the individuals involved. How prevalent are they?

Chapter Two, Profiles of a Child with Violent Tendencies, will describe a student who is likely to be violent. Currently, the nation focuses merely on the senseless tragedies of youth violence, leaving in the aftermath entire communities traumatized and victimized by brutal acts committed by children.

Our schools are joining in the ranks of our American homes, families, streets, and communities in the chronic list of bizarre, unexplainable and needless violent crimes that children as young as four years old and as old as 18 are committing.

In many cases there are overt warning signs or indicators of these violence-prone juveniles. Currently, police and educators are becoming proactive by learning to recognize and identify these children at high risk of violent behaviors.

CHAPTER TWO

Profile of a Child with Violent Tendencies

We've all seen students like this—average, a little eccentric, who have a clique of friends but are rarely in trouble. They are not considered depressed, nor are there apparent signs that they have any psychiatric disorders. Don Stone, Thurston High School's student service coordinator and school counselor in Springfield, Oregon, didn't view Kip Kinkel, the 15 year old who allegedly gunned down classmates in the school's cafeteria, as someone with violent tendencies. How do you know if a student has violent tendencies?

Dr. Pamela Riley, director for the Center of Prevention of School Violence (North Carolina), conducted a workshop for principals. She stated that violence can happen anywhere. Each school and community is unique, which is why each school's safe school strategies are different. When asked about a profile for children with violent tendencies she said generically there were certain things to look for to identify these students. Some risk factors may include living in abusive or neglectful homes or in crime-ridden neighborhoods, or being bullied or outcasts.

Eric Harris, the Columbine High School shooter, was described as a person who told jokes; he told girls they looked nice and even bought a Christmas present for a teacher. One student described him as being the greatest actor he had ever seen, a bright, smiling kid (*Denver Post*). What made him snap? Was it his rejection by the Marine Corps five days earlier? Was it a decision before the shootings to stop taking his antipsychotic drugs? Was it years of being taunted? Answers to these questions might explain the unexplainable.

Neighbors remember Eric Harris playing street hockey in front of his house. He helped the family with chores on the weekend. He always drove slowly in the neighborhood and waved to the neighbors.

What about Dylan Klebold, the other Columbine High School shooter? Dylan was viewed by classmates as having a low self-esteem. He was a follower and not a leader. It was said that he was Eric Harris' shadow. However, within the shadow a dark side emerged and took over. What was it? Both Harris and Klebold had juvenile records for breaking into a van, but they entered a diversion program that gave them a clean record. Klebold shared friendships with those other than the Trench Coat Mafia—he had athletic friends. Klebold grew up in a $400,000 home among the upper middle class. He worked in a pizza parlor and he had a family that loved him.

Michael Carneal, the West Paducah, Kentucky, shooter, was a B student and his father was a prominent attorney. From his class writings and projects, it was revealed that he felt like he was being picked on. He was small and emotionally immature but was not a discipline problem. Classmates described him as friendly. He later told law enforcement that he had no idea why he shot those three girls (according to the Associated Press).

It is estimated that 8 to 10 percent of America's population over the age of 18 years old may possess antisocial personality disorders; these persons are created from our adolescent population. The youth violence that is raging in our public schools and across the nation forces us to examine our children in an attempt to effectively resolve this tragedy.

Each day children are victims of violence and murder by other children. The nation has been most horrified and driven to action and dialogue by the most recent school killings. The results for this type of violence are unclear. Many feel that today's society provides too much stimulation, too much violence on television, and too much access to adult entertainment via the Internet. Children are exposed to these elements and they cannot process them as adults can. Neil Postman (1982, *The Disappearance of Childhood*) says, "Our children live in a society whose psychological and social contexts do not stress the differences between adults and children. As the adult world opens itself in every conceivable way to children, they will inevitably emulate adult criminal activity."

The underlying causes of violent behavior in children are varied, according to experts in children's health and psychology. We don't know how children learn violence. Children involved in the school shootings recently span a wide spectrum in terms of causes and situations where children may act out violently. Howard Spivak, M.D., a professor of pediatrics and community health at Tufts University and a member of the American Academy of Pediatrics Task Force on Violence, said the boy involved in the Springfield, Oregon, incident "was clearly a disturbed child who had been exhibiting serious psychiatric symptoms, he was a powder keg." Dr. Spivak described the Jonesboro, Arkansas, incident as different; "those kids were not exhibiting those kinds of symptoms." According to Spivak, a child who is likely to become violent will often be a bully or constantly be victimized by others; absent from school frequently; socially isolated and appearing to become more isolated; and suffering from failing grades. Often he comes from violent homes and violent communities.

When identifying characteristics or symptoms of children with violent tendencies we can never be sure how accurate they are or that we are not stereotyping. No one symptom stands out to imply a violent behavior. As parents, educators, community members and law enforcement officers, we must observe our children for certain traits. In this way we can establish a pattern of mild, moderate or severe levels of potential violence.

Why didn't we see it coming? This question has been asked many times by different groups of people. We review over and over in our minds the days leading us to the incident and the days after the incident. What did the child say? How did they act? How could we have prevented the incident?

In most cases, there are early warning signs that children who have violent tendencies will harm themselves or others; certain behavioral and emotional signs that, when viewed in context, can tell us we have a very troubled child. However, early warnings are just that—indicators that a student may need help.

Such signs may or may not indicate a serious problem. When this profile was presented to school principals, their response was: how many characteristics does a child display before I seek action? Early warning signs provide us with the impetus to check out our concerns and address the child's needs; they allow us to act responsibly by getting help for the child before problems escalate.

It's important to avoid inappropriately labeling or stigmatizing individual students because they appear to fit a specific profile or set of early warning indicators. Teachers and administrators—and other school staff—are not professionally trained to analyze children's feelings, motives and behaviors. However, they see these children every day, eight hours a day. Effective schools offer special training to identify these children who might have violent tendencies.

Educators, families and communities can increase their ability to recognize early warning signs by establishing close, caring and supportive relationships with children and youth. Unfortunately, however, there is a real danger that early warning signs can be misinterpreted. Educators, parents and community can ensure these behaviors are not misinterpreted by using several significant principles to better understand them. These principles include:

Do no harm. There are certain risks in identifying children who are troubled. The early warning signs should not be used as a reason to isolate the student, exclude, or punish them. Nor should they be used as a checklist for formally identifying, mislabeling, or stereotyping children.

Understand violence and aggression within context. Violence is contextual. Violent and aggressive behavior as an expression of emotion may have many antecedent factors—factors in the home, school and larger social environment.

Avoid stereotypes. Stereotypes can interfere and harm the school community's ability to identify and help children. It is important to be aware of false cues—including race, socioeconomics, cognitive or academic ability, or physical appearance.

View early warning signs within a developmental context. Children and youth mature at varying degrees and chronological ages. They may express their needs differently in elementary, middle and high school.

On June 13, 1999, after the tragic loss of life and injuries at Thurston High School in Springfield, Oregon, President Clinton directed the Department of Education (Secretary Richard W. Riley) and the Attorney General of the United States Department of Justice (Janet Reno) to develop an early warning guide to help "adults reach out to troubled children quickly and effectively." The early warning signs are a direct response to the presidential request and are available on the Internet.

The following list and descriptions are not to be viewed as all-inclusive but merely a beginning point for helping our children. We need to familiarize ourselves with the following profile of a student who may pose a threat to others. The list is derived from several sources including the National School Safety Center, Early Warning Signs (developed by Richard Riley and Janet Reno), and student interviews. It should again be noted that no profile can be all-inclusive. We should all be alert to other unusual or aberrant behavior or outbursts.

Has tantrums and uncontrollable anger. This is typical of immature behavior, which has been associated with violent tendencies. These outbursts are sometimes expressed frequently and intensely in response to minor irritants and may signal potential violent behavior toward self or others.

Characteristically resorts to name calling, cursing or abusive language. Sometimes children are merely imitating what they hear at home or in their communities. This could be an indicator of disrespect for authority, the opposite sex or classmates. By using abusive language, the individual can feel superior because they are "really letting you have it." Sometimes, the offensive language is used to get one's attention and can indicate the child is calling out for help. However, it can also signify that the individual is not comfortable in their environment and that they are substituting familiar words or expressions that are not suitable for use in the school or community setting.

Habitually makes a violent threat when angry. Every threat should always be taken seriously. Some schools have a no-threat policy in which students who have made threats are mandated to seek counseling before they can return to school. This policy will be addressed in Chapter Three. One of the most reliable indicators that a youth is likely to commit a dangerous act toward themselves or others is a detailed and specific threat to use violence. Recent incidents across the country clearly indicate that threats to commit violence against oneself or others should be taken very seriously. Steps must be taken to ensure the threats are not carried out.

Has previously brought a weapon to school. Children and youths who have access to firearms are at greater risk of using violence. These youths also have a higher probability of becoming victims. Families can reduce inappropriate access and use by restricting, monitoring, and supervising children's access to firearms and other weapons. Most schools have a zero tolerance for guns brought to school by students and expulsion is required. However, when these students are expelled, they are not required to participate in conflict resolution or other intervention strategies. Instead, they are normally on the street and combing the neighborhoods or communities, and still have access to guns or weapons.

Has a background of discipline problems. Chronic behavior and disciplinary problems both in the school and at home suggest that underlying emotional needs are not being met. These unmet needs may be manifested in acting out and aggressive behaviors. These problems may set the stage for the child to violate norms and rules, defy authority, disengage from school, and engage in aggressive behaviors with other children and adults. School administrators have often developed a system for tracking students with disciplinary problems; these documentations need to be reviewed on a regular basis.

Has a background of drug, alcohol or other substance abuse or dependency. These traits are extremely important because by them one can identify youths who have lost self-control. These vices also expose youth to violence, either as perpetrators, victims, or both. Youth and their behavior are drastically effected when they are under the influence of drugs or alcohol. Sometimes shy, inverted children become raging, belligerent human beings.

Has few or no close friends. In some situations, gradual and eventually complete withdrawal from social contacts can be an important indicator of a troubled child. The withdrawal often stems from feelings of depression, rejection, persecution, unworthiness, and lack of confidence. They are highly dependent on the friends they do have and tend to imitate their mannerisms and habits.

No supervision at home. "In our schools today, 70 percent of the mothers work, 43 percent qualify for ... reduced lunch and 67 percent come from dysfunctional families. Also, schools are asked to provide before and after school daycare" (Garrett, p. 93). American mothers, both those who work and those who stay at home, spend less than 30 minutes a day on the average talking to their children. This is not enough time. In 1993, a study was conducted of working parents, and in it two-thirds admitted they did not spend enough time with their children. Mothers are often not home with their children after school, and neither parent is monitoring and instructing children on the difference between right and wrong. Without instruction into what proper behavior is, without constant reminders by a supervising parent, kids will drift into trouble. Children want and need attention from their parents, and will do anything to get it—even criminal acts. When parents leave their children alone, they increase the odds that tragedy will occur.

Is preoccupied with weapons, explosives or other incendiary devices. This has proven to be one of the major characteristics of youth with violent tendencies. Every youth who committed serious acts of violence had this trait. A lot of children exhibiting this characteristic are regular "surfers" on the Internet and several have their own web page.

Displays cruelty to animals. According to school resource officers recently interviewed there is a very high correlation between cruelty to animals and acts of violence. The cruelty to animals tends to start out on a small scale and eventually leads to bigger acts and destruction. This trait has been evidenced in juveniles that engage in the chronic pattern of terrorizing, abusing or injuring other children or animals. Many serious violent offenders have histories of this destructive behavior as well during childhood.

Animal abuse is often viewed as too minor a problem; yet there is a direct correlation between children who abuse animals and those children who grow up to rape, abuse and murder human beings. Deviant behavior toward humans is often preceded by extreme cruelty to and torture of animals. Therefore, the cruelty of animals by children or even adults should be a red flag for future violent behavior. Violent tendencies often begin at an early age, and usually escalate in number of victims and in intensity of the act. If recognized at an early age things could be done to help educate and council these animal abusers to avoid future violence. Fostering a reverence for all life at an early age and changing children's views toward animals may prevent violent behavior towards animals and humans.

Has witnessed or been a victim of neglect or abuse in the home. Children who are victims of violence—including physical or sexual abuse—in the community, at school, or at home are sometimes at risk themselves of becoming violent toward themselves or others. Again, some of the children are merely reproducing what they experience in their homes and communities.

Feelings of being picked on or persecuted. The youth who feels constantly picked on, teased, bullied, singled out for ridicule, and humiliated at home or school may initially withdraw socially. If not given adequate support in curtailing these feelings, some children may vent them in inappropriate aggression or violence. These youngsters may have a tendency to demonstrate these feelings to others.

Tends to blame others for difficulties and problems they cause. This characteristic is very common among children who have the tendency for violent behaviors. Warning signals should appear when youngsters do not feel remorse, guilt, shame, anxiety, or a sense of wrongdoing for engaging in violent behaviors. Many tend to place the blame for their behaviors on their home environment, living conditions, socioeconomic status and other such variables.

Consistently prefers television shows, reading materials, movies or music expressing violent themes, rituals and abuse. The average elementary age child spends 30 hours per week viewing television. By 16, the average child will have witnessed 200,000 acts of violence and by 18, approximately 40,000 sexually explicit scenes (Garrett, p. 99). Children become immune to violence because they have watched so much television. A very popular medium is the Internet; most children are not supervised when they explore it. This can result in them gaining access to unsuitable web sites and viewing violence. Some youth even have their own web page in which they keep "mission logs" or violent tasks they will accomplish. There is definitely a direct correlation between the Internet and violence. Also, playing violent video games where players use guns to kill creatures is a definite characteristic of violent tendencies. In addition, music that spews hate rhetoric is a frequent indicator of a troubled youth.

There are three major concerns regarding the effects of television violence identified by the National Association for the Education of Young Children (1990):

1. Children may become less sensitive to the pain and suffering of others.

2. They may be more likely to behave in aggressive or harmful ways toward others.

3. They may become more fearful of the world around them.

Another concern is that fearful children who are viewers of violence learn that aggression is a successful and acceptable way to achieve goals and solve problems; they are less likely to benefit from creative play, imaginative play, as the natural means to express feelings, overcome anger and gain self-control.

Obsessed with military paraphernalia. This obsession is evident with the fascination for guns and explosives and the playing of military games, either on video or through "acting out." The trait might include a fascination with rocket launchers, grenades, and shotguns. Dressing in military attire can be linked to this fascination with the military.

Reflects anger, frustration, and the dark side of life in school writings, drawings or projects. In the Columbine shooting, the shooters had made a video reflecting miming guns with their hands. If frequent violent themes are used in student writings or drawings this could indicate a tendency for violence. Children and youth often express their thoughts, feelings, desires and intentions in their drawings and in stories, poetry and other writings. Many children produce work about violent themes that for the most part is harmless when taken in context. However, an oversimplification of violence in writings and drawings that is directed at specific individuals consistently, over time, may signal emotional problems and the potential for violence.

Is involved with a gang or an antisocial group on the fringe of peer acceptance. Gangs that support antisocial values and behaviors—including extortion, intimidation, and acts of violence toward other students—cause fear and stress among other students. Youth who are readily influenced may adopt these values and act in certain violent or aggressive ways. Gang-related and turf battles are common occurrences tied to the use of drugs and often result in injury or death.

Uncontrollable rage. Anger can be a natural emotion or response. However, anger that is expressed frequently and intensely in response to minor situations may signal potential violent behavior toward self or others. If this is a common occurrence, opportunities for anger management should be made readily available to the youth

Patterns of impulsive and chronic hitting, intimidating and bullying behaviors. Youth often engage in acts of shoving and aggression. However, some mildly aggressive behaviors such as constant hitting and bullying of others that occur early in children's lives, if left unattended, can escalate into more serious behaviors.

Past history of violent and aggressive behavior. Unless provided with support and counseling, a youth who has a history of aggressive behaviors is likely to repeat these behaviors. Aggressive and violent acts may be directed toward other individuals, be expressed in cruelty to animals, or include fire setting. Youths who show an early pattern of antisocial behavior frequently and across multiple settings are particularly at risk for future aggression and antisocial behavior. Similarly, youths who engage in overt behaviors such as bullying, generalized aggression and defiance, and covert behaviors such as stealing, vandalism, lying, cheating and fire setting also are at risk for more serious aggressive behavior. The age of onset may be a key factor in interpreting early warning signs. For example, children who engage in aggression and drug abuse at an early age (before 12) are more likely to show violence later on than are children who begin such behavior at an older age. In the presence of such signs it is important to review the child's history with behavioral experts and seek parents' observations and insights.

Violence is okay. This is a serious problem among youth because they view acts of violence as being acceptable. They generally will resolve their conflicts with violence rather than mediation or practicing appropriate communication skills.

No remorse. This individual typically lacks a conscience or has an underdeveloped conscience. Warning signs might include a lack of remorse, guilt, shame, anxiety or sense of wrongdoing for engaging in socially unacceptable behaviors. These people do not see themselves as being wrong. They practice deception, manipulation, exploitation, theft, con artistry, and various forms of abuse or violent patterns against others. A person without a conscience is usually a social misfit, the social predator, and some develop into disturbed children, or antisocial or psychopathic personalities.

Fire setting. Frequently children acting out their anger demonstrate patterns of fire-setting episodes. At one time or the other, we have all been fascinated with matches, candles and fire. However, some children employ fire to punish, torture or kill targeted victims such as parents, teachers, principals, or others whom they believe have victimized them.

Brooding. Usually these children do not understand the importance of forgiving others; they tend to live in the past, focusing on past injustices, holding grudges which feed their anger and rage. A typical characteristic of this child is being seemingly withdrawn and quiet.

Self-inflicted wounds. Frequently serious cases of children demonstrating high levels of violent behaviors exhibit various self-inflicted wounds. Such wounds can range from homemade tattoos to broken limbs.

Collecting weapons. Many troubled juveniles participating in school and family violence are fascinated with weapons and collect them. Weapons include firearms, ammunition, knives, bomb-making information and materials for incendiary explosives. It's very common for this kind of child to steal or remove items from family, friends and neighbors. The Internet has proved to be a very popular source for getting recipes for bombs or explosives.

Irresponsibility. These youths avoid responsibility at all cost. They may exhibit chronic patterns of blame shifting, excuse making and distorting the facts to accommodate their avoidance of being held accountable for wrongdoing, which includes violent behavior.

Social withdrawal. In some situations, gradual and eventually complete withdrawal from social contacts can be an important indicator of a troubled child. The withdrawal often stems from feelings of depression, rejection, persecution, unworthiness, and a lack of confidence.

Feelings of isolation. Research has shown that the majority of children who are isolated and appear to be friendless are not violent. In fact, these feelings are sometimes characteristic of children and youths who may be troubled, withdrawn or have internal issues that hinder the development of social affiliations. However, other research has shown that in some cases feelings of isolation and not having friends are associated with children who behave aggressively and violently.

Low school interest and poor academic performance. Poor school achievement can be the result of many factors. It is important to consider whether there is a drastic change in performance or whether poor performance, if it becomes a chronic condition, limits the child's capacity to learn. In some situations, acting out and aggressive behaviors may occur. It is important to assess the emotional and cognitive reasons for the academic performance change to determine the true nature of the problem.

The children convicted or accused in the high-profile episodes of school violence over the past couple of years had several things in common. They tended to be loners picked on by other children. They were of normal or above average intelligence. Most had spoken of committing a violent act before the shootings. Some of the accused shooters came from broken homes. In at least two cases, the boys were accused of shooting and killing their parents before or after the school shootings.

According to Spivak (1996), a child who becomes violent will often be a bully or chronically victimized; absent from school often; socially isolated and appearing to become more isolated; and suffering failing grades at school. They often come from violent homes and from violent communities.

"This recent series of killings in our schools has seared the heart of America about as much as anything I can remember in a long, long time" (President Bill Clinton, television interview, July 7, 1999).

The following are fictitious profiles of youth who are at risk of violent behaviors:

Profile: Bob Doe, 18 years old

School Bob lives in a middle class neighborhood with both of his biological parents. He has a local job at the carwash and owns his own automobile. He is always telling jokes and funny stories. Bob is courteous and has nice manners. Recently the university of his choice rejected him. He was fascinated by the military and planned to get a college degree and then enter the military as an officer, hopefully in the division of weaponry. He attended the prom with a girl he met on the Internet and later she broke up with him. The break-up made him furious especially when the girl started dating one of the football players. He continued to have violent feelings toward the football player. The crowd he started to hang with were considered losers or outcasts—they did not fit into any social clique. He loved video games, especially Doom. In his junior year he vandalized a neighbor's house and grounds. He attended a juvenile training program. He became more and more enraged and hated kids of different races. His grades were failing and his parents were asked to attend a conference.

Domestic Love-hate relationship with parents—lately more hate than love. Hates younger brother and is constantly hitting him, pushing and bullying the sibling. Makes excuses for his behavior toward his brother. Erupts violently for no apparent reasons and retreats to his room. He does not allow his parents or brother to enter his bedroom.

Profile: Joe, 16 years old

School Constantly being picked on because of his small body frame. Does not participate in sports and is not in any social cliques. He is often referred to as a nerd because he is very bright and made a 1500 on his SAT. Has a keen interest in weapons and is constantly researching this topic on the Internet. Is well liked by teachers and staff because of his high academic standards and his meek disposition. Has no interest in the opposite sex.

Domestic He lives with his mother and stepbrother. There is no male figure in the household. Mother works double shifts and is seldom home. He is responsible for the after school care of the younger stepbrother. His stepbrother is seven and is constantly mistreated by Joe. Joe threatens bodily harm if little brother tells mom about the misbehavior. He spends all of his extra time on the Internet and has found some very interesting web pages on explosives, guns and how to make a bomb. Recently, he found the recipe for a tennis ball bomb.

Profile: Michael, 14 years old

School   Is not passing any of his core or encore courses. He has been retained once for not performing on grade level and spends a lot of time in the principal's office for fighting, cursing and other inappropriate behavior. He thinks it's not really his fault; the principal and the teachers don't like him—they never have. Latest school incident was skipping school—his father has to come to school. He will be suspended for seven days after the parent conference. Michael said his father would beat him this time for his behavior. He hates everyone—especially blacks. He constantly taunts them by name-calling and often writes "Nigger go home" on the bathroom and hallway walls. He attends counseling weekly because of his previous juvenile record (he assaulted a teacher) but merely sits through the session brooding over having to attend "the dumb old thing."

Domestic   Lives on the "wrong" side of town. Comes home daily to an empty house. His mother abandoned him when he was eight years old. His father is an alcoholic. He hangs with a gang called the "Rebels." His dad is seldom home because he's out with his pals. When his dad is home, he's usually got a lot of friends with him; they sit around the house drinking and playing poker. When his dad gets drunk, he's always in a rage and takes it out on his son. His dad thinks if he could just get that one break in life, he would be okay. Meals are normally fast food or from cans or boxes. Michael qualifies for free lunch at school but his dad won't let him accept it.

Profile: Sam, 13 years old

School   Hates school. Constantly brags about cutting up squirrels and cats, and claims to have set fire to a dog. Has been charged with throwing rocks and breaking out a neighbor's car window. Has been suspended from school six times this year for cursing and disrespect to teachers and administrators. Was recommended for a community program that is supposed to help troubled youth but his parents would not let him participate. Has very few friends. His only friend is an eleven year old who looks up to him. Smokes frequently at school and has even brought alcohol to school but has never been caught. Wears camouflage fatigues daily and combat boots. Has a homemade tattoo—a Nazi symbol on his right forearm. At a recent school dance, he threw water balloons on the kids as they entered the gym and imitated shooting them.

Domestic Comes from a well-to-do family—both parents have professional jobs. He is an only child. Purchases new video games weekly—enjoys video games with violence and shooting. He can "con" his parents into believing just about anything—nothing is ever his fault. Parents are constantly threatening to sue the school for discriminating against their child and not treating him fairly. Parents never spend time with him—when they are not at work they are on leisure vacations. Sam never goes on vacation with them. Instead, when the parents are gone, he "parties," inviting older kids to his house. The older kids come to his house because of the free booze and food.

Profile: Jim, 17 years old

School Has academic problems although he has a high IQ—he is an underachiever. He is very confrontational with teachers. He has attended six schools because his mother moves a lot. Has a lot of disciplinary problems—cannot get along with peers or adults. He picks fights frequently.

Domestic Always threatening to burn the house down if he doesn't get his way. Very abusive to mother and younger siblings—he broke his younger brother's arm because he wouldn't give him the remote control for the television. Destroys property frequently—he recently cut his mother's coat into shreds because she wouldn't give him money for cigarettes. Smokes, and mother can't make him stop. Mother admits she can't do anything with him. When the school calls because of his behavior, she tells them he's their problem from 8:00 until 3:00 each day. Has stolen mother's car twice and gone joyriding—mother did not call the police. Never shows remorse for his actions—the only time he displays emotion is when he looks at a picture of his dad in his naval uniform; his dad was killed in the line of duty. Hates all Asians—they killed his dad. At school he calls them "High Yellers."

Johns Hopkins Study

A Johns Hopkins School of Public Health study reveals that a teenager's ability to interact with family and friends and whether they participate in school can show the presence of psychiatric disorders much earlier than traditional signs—such as police run-ins or school failure. Boys with psychiatric disorders were found to have significant academic problems, troubled relationships with family and friends, and were not accepted by their peers.

There were differences in social behavior between healthy girls and girls with disorders, the study found.

If a child has risk factors, violent behavior can be avoided if the child learns to communicate and empathize with others, think broadly, identify alternative solutions and control their impulses. The number one key is for children to have a positive role model in their lives, such as a parent, coach, teacher or minister.

In late May, an angry, revengeful 15-year-old student, Kipland Kinkel, allegedly murdered his parents in cold blood, then drove to Thurston High School in Springfield, Oregon. He went to the school cafeteria and opened fire with a semiautomatic rifle and two pistols, discharging 51 rounds of ammunition. He wounded 25 classmates before he was wrestled to the floor and held until law enforcement arrived.

Kip had previously bragged about cutting animals up and blowing up a dead cow. He had been charged with throwing rocks at cars as they passed under a freeway bridge. Before the shooting spree, Kip had been arrested, charged with possession of a stolen firearm on school property and expelled from school. After his arrest, the police found a grenade, several bombs and other incriminating evidence at his parents' home. In his yearbook, his classmates labeled him "Most Likely to Start World War III."

This is *only one* incident that reflects something is wrong with our children. What is wrong with a society that produces young people capable of shooting their own classmates in premeditated, cold-blooded murder?

Not long before, a similar massacre in Jonesboro, Arkansas, dominated headlines throughout the United States and throughout the world. The April 6, 1998, edition of America's three leading news magazines all gave important coverage. The cover of *Time* displayed a picture of 11-year-old Andrew Golden—dressed in camouflage and holding a rifle—with the words "Armed and Dangerous" written across it. The magazine's featured article, titled "The Hunter and the Choir Boy," began by talking about the two boys and their different lifestyles. How did childish games and grudges turn into an American tragedy? *Time* also featured another article, "Toward the Root of the Evil Problem."

Newsweek's April 6, 1998, cover showed Jonesboro's 13-year-old Mitchell Johnson holding a pistol in front of his chest, with the caption "The Schoolyard Killers." Its article was entitled "The Boys Behind the Ambush."

So what's really the cause of these killings and violent incidents across our nation? What causes children as young as 11 to embark on a killing spree? How do little boys turn into criminals? Allegedly, Mitch Johnson used cocaine. According to interviews with his classmates, he was a real bully. His parents were divorced and his girlfriend had recently broken up with him. Any or all of these factors could have contributed to the Jonesboro nightmare. On the other hand, Andrew Golden came from a solid family, but he may have succumbed to peer pressure or societal influence.

Children as young as preschoolers can show violent behavior. Although parents and adults who witness this behavior may be concerned, they think their children will grow out of it. Violent behavior in a child at any age needs to be taken seriously. It should not be merely dismissed as a phase they are going through.

Children who have been identified as having several of the indicators from the profile should be carefully evaluated. Parents and educators should be careful not to minimize these behaviors in children.

What Can Be Done If a Child Shows Violent Behavior?

A parent or other adult should immediately arrange for a complete comprehensive evaluation conducted by a qualified mental health professional. Early treatment by a professional can assist in helping children overcome violent tendencies, and such treatment can be obtained through the programs offered by any adolescent services. The goals of treatment typically focus on helping the child learn how to control their anger; to express anger and frustrations in appropriate ways; to accept responsibility for their actions; and to accept consequences. In addition, family conflicts, school problems, and community issues must be addressed.

Can Anything Prevent Tendencies of Violent Behavior in Children?

Research demonstrates that much violent behavior can be decreased if the characteristics of a child with violent tendencies are reduced or eliminated. Most importantly, efforts should be directed at decreasing the exposure of children and adolescents to violence in the home, the community, and the media. Violence leads to violence.

The development of chronic aggressive violent behavior is complex and appears to involve the interplay of multiple risk factors. These include individual factors such as genetics, or physiological abnormalities. Factors relating to family functioning, peer associations, and the community in which the child resides probably account for the greatest variation in the learning and expression of aggression and violence.

From Rick Van Acker's presentation at the T/TAC Conference, "Challenging Behavior: Making Our Schools Safe Again," May 1, 1997, and on his web page, he gives five specific conditions that have shown empirically to be most conducive to the learning and maintenance of aggression. The conditions include:

- The child is provided many opportunities to observe aggression.
- The child is the object of aggression.
- The child is given few opportunities to develop positive social bonds with others.
- The child is reinforced in their aggression.
- The child associates with other individuals who engage in and encourage aggression and violent behavior.

Early Intervention

If we examine the ages at which children and youth begin to develop serious aggressive and violent behavior, we can clearly identify two distinct pathways. Children who demonstrate noncompliance and aggressive behavior very early in their development indicate the first and most serious pathway. For many of these children, aggressiveness becomes a relatively stable behavioral response between four and nine years of age. There also exists a higher probability that these individuals will continue their aggressive and violent behaviors well into adulthood. An estimated five to eight percent of males and three to six percent of females display this pattern of development.

The second pathway, involving the greater number of children or youth, is characterized by time-limited violence and aggression displayed during adolescence. Aggressive and violent behavior is relatively common among adolescents. It is estimated that between 20 percent and 40 percent of males and 4 percent to 15 percent of females report participating in one or more serious acts of violence. Typically, youth begin to initiate these aggressive and violent behaviors following 12 years of age with the highest risk of initiation between 15 and 16 year of age. Participation in aggressive and violent behavior for the majority of these youth drops drastically after age 17.

Schools must provide intervention services to help prevent serious aggressive and violent behavior during the early school years and continue intervention throughout the developmental years. Efforts should be provided at two levels. Primary intervention programs, including general emotion recognition, anger management, and conflict resolution strategies could be provided for all students. More intense preventive and treatment programs need to involve family members, and should be developed and delivered to students specifically identified as at-risk for the development of violent tendencies.

Theodore Roosevelt once stated, "To educate a person in mind and not morals is to create a menace to society."

Many of today's children receive no or very little guidance from their parents. Fewer community members are taking a look at our children and fewer are attempting to help them. Instead our children learn about values and morals from television, media and peers. Knowing this, what can educators, parents and community do? We need to build a culture and model the behavior we want our children to emulate. In addition, schools must develop cooperative partnerships with parents, community and law enforcement.

Character education can be a key to a learning community and to gaining public support. Teaching good character is initially the responsibility of parents and is only then supported by the schools: parents are the children's first moral teachers. The schools need to address moral knowing, moral feeling, and moral behavior. Character education is moral values in action. They need to stress knowing the good habits of the mind, habits of the heart and doing good. Good character education is based on universal moral values. There is no such thing as a value-free school—teaching is value-loaded.

One of our biggest responsibilities is to help children develop habits of self-discipline and respect that constitutes character. Hillary Clinton's *It Takes a Village* offers both personal and national examples of the need for building character in our children. "When it comes to everyday life, however, parents have to concentrate on instilling self-discipline, self-control, and self-respect early on, and then must follow their children to practice those skills the way they would let them exercise their muscles or brains" (www.hillary2000.org/).

Killer kids. They're everywhere these days, or so it seems. Probably no group in America today inspires more fear than the teenagers regularly featured on the evening news. What many find most frightening about these young murderers is that their crimes seem so senseless and random. Thus, after each bizarre slaying, the search is on for an explanation.

Sometimes we blame a movie, as in the West Paducah, Kentucky, school shooting; the Lillelid family massacre in Johnson City, Tennessee,was said to have stemmed from Oliver Stone's *Natural Born Killers*. Sometimes we blame the gun: if only the teenager hadn't had one, this wouldn't have happened. Sometimes we blame Satanism, as in a Mississippi school shooting. We've also blamed rock (and rap) lyrics, the board game Dungeons and Dragons, and the Internet.

None of these explanations can be held solely responsible for the violence that has taken place involving kids. Movies, games, music and the Internet may be variables but the entire blame cannot be placed on these objects.

A 1996 Harvard study of guns and gang murders found both juvenile and adult murderers to have a long record of serious crimes. Substance abusers, people with above average intelligence and those with mental disorders are several times more likely to commit violent crimes than are ordinary citizens.

Teen killers tend to have a very narrow view of other people's rights. They also have encountered time and time again a feeling that the only way to deal with their frustration and despair is to bring it to a climactic conclusion.

The reason so many teens are becoming dangerous killers is that the social safeguards that used to exist are failing. Our society is changing at a very rapid pace. Families, churches, schools, child welfare authorities, courts, mental health organizations, are all becoming less and less effective at keeping these potential killers from reaching their final, lethal stage. We are all paying the price and blaming Oliver Stone or the Internet—this will not help us create a solution to stop the killings.

Dr. Helen Smith, a forensic psychologist specializing in violent children, gave testimony before the Ad Hoc Committee on School Violence (April 21, 1999), and recommended the following:

- Place children in an alternative program for observation for a 30-day period if they bring guns or weapons to school. Today most schools have a zero tolerance and students are expelled for up to 365 days, but an alternative placement is not an option.
- Make counseling and psychotherapy more available in our schools. Much of the funding for counseling has been reduced in the schools due to budget decreases.
- Provide long-term parenting programs for high-risk families and

short-term programs for all families of school-age children. These preventive programs need to focus on teaching parents about what is appropriate behavior for healthy adolescents as opposed to concentrating on those who are depressed or aggressive.

- Violence-prevention programs are needed for children. Education is the key in helping students to identify other potentially dangerous students. There have been school tragedies averted by other students telling school officials that someone has brought weapons or explosives to school and school officials acting on the potential threat.

- Inservice programs for teachers and staff. Educators may not always recognize the symptoms of at-risk children or those with violent tendencies.

- Critical thinking skills. There is a high correlation between youth impulsiveness and a teenager's frantic brain activity in the amygdala. Older teens and adults show more activity in the rational frontal lobe—the brain tissue involved in planning, insight and organization. We need to encourage young teenagers to develop the frontal lobe by teaching them to think more rationally.

While it is difficult to generalize about all school-related teen killers, there do appear some common characteristics about them. The common link seems to be that in each killing, there has been a feeling on the part of the teenager that he could not express in words the depth of his true feelings of rage as a result of feeling rejected or hurt or stressed. In a letter, Luke Woodham, the 16-year-old youth who shot up a school in Pearl, Mississippi, indicates the depth of his rage: "I am not insane. I am angry. I killed because people like me are mistreated everyday. I did this to show society if they push us, we push back" (*http://www.violentkids.com/articles/violence article1.html*). In most of the school killings, the killers also wrote a note about their intentions or told someone of the intended crime. Generally, school killers do not strike without warning. Usually, they leave clues that announce what they are planning, well in advance of their crimes.

The problem is, all too often, no one is listening. In order to understand the minds of teen killers, one must understand how they think. To be rejected or considered a nobody is often worse than death. They prey upon us because we have turned a deaf ear. How much easier it might have been had someone taken more seriously the note Luke Woodham gave a classmate detailing his intentions.

Factors contributing to school violence are numerous, complex and mostly community-related. Teachers perceive that the major factors contributing to student violence are lack of parental supervision at home (71 percent), lack of family involvement with the school (66 percent) and exposure to violence in the mass media (55 percent).

In too many communities, children constantly send signals that they feel isolated from society. These feelings know no geographical, social or economic boundaries. Increasingly, many youths come from communities where the vast majority of the experiences to which they have been exposed have been hostile. They have had to fight to survive. These young men and women are filled with rage and a sense of rejection and, as a result, do not believe that they owe society anything.

At the same time, an increasing number of students who have grown up in mean, hostile environments are involved in acts of violence. They often cite boredom or the excitement of control as reasons for their actions. It is difficult to understand their rebellion against society.

A much more pressing issue for those concerned about the safety of children in America is the threat of everyday gun violence. As many as eight children a day are killed by guns, mostly by adults. Children are killed everyday in gun accidents at 23 times the rate at which they are killed in schools. According to the Centers for Disease Control, children in America are 12 times more likely to die from guns than children in 25 other industrialized countries, including Israel and Northern Ireland. While killings by juveniles with guns quadrupled from 1984 to 1994, nongun killings by youth stayed the same. Simply stated, the entire increase in juvenile homicides between 1984 and 1994 was gun-related. While America has a homicide rate among its adults and juveniles which is still too high, the good news from this report is that our nation's school children are well protected from homicides during school hours. Despite the recent shocking school shootings throughout the country, America's public schools remain safe. The likelihood of being killed in a school-associated violence is slightly less than one in a million. The chance of a child being violently killed by an adult in their own home or somewhere other than school is far greater. Statistically, as both students and principals have reported, crime does not dominate the school. Rather than search for policies to make already schools safer, we should seek to channel the public energy created by these shootings into taking guns out of the hands of children and adults, and providing constructive opportunities for children during peek crime hours.

One way to reduce criminal activity among youth is to provide enriched afterschool activities. Again and again studies have demonstrated that afterschool recreational programs which aggressively recruit youth and sustain participation in their programs hold excellent potential to prevent juvenile delinquency within the community.

The problem of violent children will more than likely get worse before it gets better. The cultural, social and familial factors that led to these shootings of young people killing their parents, teachers and classmates over the last few years did not miraculously disappear over the summer, and will likely result in equally tragic consequences in the future—perhaps even more frequently.

We do not know how children learn violence or even if this behavior is a learned trait. The children involved in the shooting tragedies are the product of a wide spectrum of causes and situations where children may act out violently. We teach children to use violence and we live in a cultural society that almost promotes violence as a means of coping with anger. How many times have we heard parents tell their children, you have to stick up for yourself—if he hits you, you hit him back. Also, when parents are called to schools because of their children fighting, it is common to hear, "I told him not to take anything else off that kid—and to stick up for himself." As a society we are shocked and outraged when children act out violently.

Pam Riley (Center for the Prevention of Violence in North Carolina) outlines some positive things that build resiliency in students and that schools can instill in students. They include: Creating strong bonds between family, school and community; developing opportunities for meaningful involvement in family, school and community; developing social competence skills and problem-solving skills; giving recognition in the form of clear expectations; and giving recognition to students in the form of rewards and incentives for positive behavior.

Children Who May Have Violent Tendencies

A checklist developed from the previous profiles and from characteristics of children with violent tendencies includes:

1. Has a history of tantrums and uncontrollable angry outbursts.
2. Characteristically resorts to name calling, cursing or abusive language.

3. Habitually makes violent threats when angry.

4. Has previously brought a weapon to school.

5. Has a background of serious disciplinary problems at school and in the community.

6. Has a background of drug, alcohol or other substance abuse or dependency.

7. Is on the fringe of their peer group with no close friends.

8. Is preoccupied with weapons, explosives or other incendiary devices.

9. Has previously been truant, suspended or expelled from school.

10. Displays cruelty to animals.

11. Has little or no supervision and support from parents or a caring adult.

12. Has witnessed or been a victim of abuse or neglect in the home.

13. Has been bullied or bullies peers or younger children.

14. Tends to blame others for difficulties and problems.

15. Consistently prefers television shows, movies or music that express violent themes.

16. Prefers reading materials that reflect violent themes, rituals and abuse.

17. Reflects anger, frustration and the dark side of life in school essays, doodlings or drawings.

18. Is involved with a gang or cult.

19. Has been cruel to animals.

20. Is fascinated with fire and fire setting.

Each item on the checklist is valued at five points. Five to 20 points—Indicates potential violence. Twenty-five to 50 points—Child is definitely at risk and immediate intervention needs to take place. Fifty-five to 100 points—Child and his family are in immediate danger of harm being inflicted on children or family. A request needs to be made to social services and law enforcement. Professional help is required.

How Can We Intervene Effectively?

The urge to prevent further school shootings and violence has led to a proliferation of antiviolence interventions for children, youth and their families. Those programs that have been evaluated and show promise include interventions aimed at reducing risk factors or at strengthening families and children to help them resist the effects of detrimental life circumstances.

Effective intervention programs share two primary characteristics: (a) they draw on the understanding of developmental and sociocultural risk factors of antisocial behavior; and (b) they use theory-based intervention strategies with known efficacy in changing behavior, tested program designs, and validated, objective measurement techniques to assess outcomes. Other key criteria that describe the most promising intervention approaches include the following:

- They begin as early as possible. Evidence indicates that intervention early in childhood can reduce aggression and antisocial behavior.
- They address aggression as part of a constellation of antisocial behaviors in the child or youth. Aggression is the number one problem behavior found in the aggressive child. Often the cluster includes academic difficulties, poor interpersonal relationships, cognitive deficiencies, and attribution biases.
- They include multiple components that reinforce each other across the child's everyday social contexts: family, school, peer groups, media and community. Aggressive tendencies are displayed within the different components.
- They take advantage of developmental windows of opportunities: points at which interventions are especially needed or likely to make a difference. Windows should include transitions in a child's life: birth, entry into preschool, the beginning of elementary or middle school, and adolescence. The developmental challenges of adolescence are a particular window of opportunity, because the limits-testing and other age-appropriate behaviors of adolescents tend to challenge even a functional family's well-developed patterns of interaction.

Primary Prevention Programs

Prevention directed early in life can reduce factors that increase risk for antisocial behavior and clinical dysfunction in childhood and adolescence. Among the most promising interventions are:

Home visitor programs for at-risk families, which include prenatal and postnatal counseling and continued contact with the family and child in the first few years of life. In a 20-year follow-up of one such program positive results could be seen both for the child and mother (APA Commission on Violence and Youth, 1993).

Preschool programs that address diverse intellectual, emotional, and social needs and the development of cognition and decision-making processes. Two good examples of these programs include Smart Start and Title I Pre-Kindergarten. Smart Start is supported greatly by Governor Easley in North Carolina and focuses entirely on the parenting and home aspects. Title I has an excellent parent component in which parents are required to participate if their children are eligible. For the Title I classes 16 children are selected who are educationally deprived.

School-based primary prevention programs for children and adolescents are effective with children and youth that are not seriously violence-prone, but these programs have not yet been demonstrated to have major effects on seriously and persistently aggressive behavior. Evaluations on such school-based programs show they can improve prosocial competence and reduce at-risk behavior among youth who are not seriously violence-prone by promoting nonviolent norms, lessening the opportunity for and elicitation of violent acts, and preventing the sporadic aggressiveness that engages temporarily during adolescence. The program teaches youth how to cope better with the transitional crisis of adolescence and offer them alternatives and institutional constraints to keep sporadic aggressiveness within socially defined bounds. Examples of these programs include teaching about adolescence, which is typically done in fifth and sixth grades and normally occurs during health classes. The focus is on body changes and the social and emotional aspects of the changes. Other programs might be Project Pursuit or Soaring High. Both of these programs focus on team building skills, trust and socially accepted behaviors.

Secondary Prevention Programs for High-Risk Children

Secondary prevention programs that focus on improving individual affective, cognitive, and behavior skills or on modifying the learning conditions for aggression offer promise of interrupting the path toward violence for high-risk or predelinquent youth. To the extent that development is an ongoing process, programs that target learning contexts, such as the family, should produce the most long-term effects.

However, programs for youth that deal with aggressive behaviors have not been successful when they have been unfocused and not based on sound theory. Furthermore, because most programs have been relatively brief and have emphasized psychoeducational interventions, it is not known whether they would be effective with seriously aggressive or delinquent youth.

Programs that attempt to work with and modify the family system of a high-risk child have great potential to prevent the development of aggressive and violent behavior. Family variables are very important in the development and treatment of antisocial and violent behavior. For example, adolescents referred to juvenile court for minor infractions received an intervention with a family-therapy approach to identify maladaptive family interaction patterns; instruction for remedial family management skills was successful in reducing violence rates for up to 18 months. The counseling sessions dealt with parenting skills, setting parameters and getting assistance from professionals when it was necessary.

According to a report released by the Senate Judiciary Committee, the United States is now considered to be the most violent and self-destructive nation in the industrialized world. Domestic violence, assault, homicide, child abuse and neglect have become common characteristics of American life.

School crime and violence can be viewed as the tangible expression of unresolved conflict. If we empower young people and the adults who serve them with more effective conflict management skills, a more productive learning climate will result. When young people develop and apply nonviolent problem-solving skills, campus life can be dramatically improved.

When teachers and administrators train students in nonviolent problem-solving techniques, the working atmosphere among members of staff is often enhanced as a program by-product. When youth-serving agencies utilize these same skills and practices, a spirit of community cooperation and goodwill can emerge. Good conflict resolution skills, like violence, are contagious.

Infusing conflict management training into the curriculum offers hope to students and staff alike. Conflict management programs help children develop better behavioral skills, minimizing their opportunities for trouble and maximizing their opportunities for positive social interaction.

By intervening early, we stand a much better chance of providing young people with positive educational experiences that can provide the foundation for ongoing success. Educators no longer have a choice as to whether or not schools should be made safer and better for young people. It is imperative that we do everything in our power to create a climate that supports the safety, success and development of all children. The following programs emphasize effective conflict resolution skills.

Violence Prevention Programs

The following are programs that have been successful in working with children at-risk and their families:

Teach—This center in Clyde, North Carolina, has 40 trained volunteers. The organization deals with students at risk and their families. It offers a 24-hour hotline and topics range from threats or threatening situations to suicide.

Conflict Mediation Program—The Conflict Mediation Program trains teachers and students together. The program involves 45 hours of training throughout the year for 12 students, six teachers and two counselors. Certification renewal is offered for teachers. Training sessions cover communications and conflict-resolution skills, including listening; conflict styles; communication barriers; negotiating; assertive refusals; cultural diversity issues; confidentiality; and the mediation process. The mediation involves trained student mediators, an adult mediator, and two students in conflict who agree to the process. No administrators are present.

Peer Helpers—Several high schools around the country provide peer helpers. These students are selected based on their academic performance and interpersonal skills. They complete a training period conducted by school counselors or the school system's student services coordinator. They work with their peers on homework and other academic areas and conflict resolution.

Resolving Conflict Creatively Program (RCCP)—RCCP is a comprehensive program that teaches about 50,000 youth in New York schools. Regular classroom teachers teach the curriculum, and each teacher receives 20 hours of professional training from RCCP staff. The program concentrates on teaching key component skills of conflict resolution: active listening, assertiveness, expression of feelings, perspective taking, cooperation, negotiation, and ways of interrupting expressions of bias or prejudice.

A student mediation program is started in schools that have been participating in RCCP for a year. The emphasis on student mediation as part of a larger schoolwide effort is considered a significant strength over mediation by projects. A parent involvement program has recently been added as a vital component. The program trains teams of two or three parents for 60 hours to lead workshops for other parents on intergroup relations, family communications and conflict resolution.

School Conflict Management Demonstration Project—The Ohio Commission on Dispute Resolution and Conflict Management was created by the Ohio General Assembly to be a catalyst for implementing conflict management programs in Ohio's courts, state and local government, communities and colleges, and universities. Begun in 1990, the School Demonstration Project was initiated to evaluate how conflict management programs affect students and school climate. Each school submitted a plan for creating in-school training and materials needed. A planning committee was formed at each site to conduct an assessment of the school's needs and types of conflict management. Both peer mediation and conflict resolution are provided for all students.

Broader Urban Involvement and Leadership Development—BUILD is a nonprofit organization in Chicago that works with gang-affiliated youth and potential gang recruits to redirect their behavior for a positive and productive life. The program's three components are: remediation, prevention and community resource development. The remediation includes working with 20 older adolescent street gang members, helping them to find alternatives, such as employment, job training, education or practical communication skills. The preventive component is designed to work among seventh and eighth graders who have been identified by the school as being at risk of being recruited by gang members. Community resource development, the third component, works with local adult community groups, helping to mobilize, coordinate and encourage them to direct their energies toward helping youth.

Positive Alternative Gang Education—Hawaii students who miss four hours or more of school without a valid reason are required to attend a four-hour session on Saturday with their parents. Failure to attend the program may lead to stiff penalties, including arrest for truancy, police counseling or referral to family court. The program helps keep students in school, and juvenile crime and gang activity are reduced as a result. The Saturday classes inform students and their parents about the law; increase decision making and critical thinking skills; improve self-esteem; and include activities designed to help students reconnect with school.

Center for Civic Education—This center, located in Calabasas, California, offers a wide range of curricular, teacher-training and community-based programs. The principal goals of the program are to help students develop an increased understanding of the institutions of American constitutional democracy and the fundamental principles and values upon which they are founded; the skills necessary to participate as effective and responsible citizens; and the willingness to use democratic procedures for making decisions and managing conflict. The program features cooperative learning and problem-solving activities, enhances critical thinking skills, and focuses on contemporary issues and current events.

Star—This program was developed to improve race relations and foster respect for diversity among young people. It encourages youth commitment to public service by using college students as role models. In North Carolina, where the program originated four years ago, the volunteers comprise students from 22 North Carolina colleges and universities. These volunteers encourage public school students to examine their attitudes about race, ethnicity and culture. The volunteers facilitate a series of discussions among students about human relations, citizenship and community service. The college students are prepared for this task through training and educational materials developed by People for the American Way.

VISIONS—Valuable Insights and Skills to Increase Opportunities Needed to Succeed is a youth leadership development program that uses University of Georgia extension service staff and trained resident association volunteers to serve 35 selected high school youths from 10 sites in Macon. The VISION participants receive specific training and are exposed to the broader world around them through visits to the legislature, colleges and cultural events. All participants receive educational guidance and career counseling to help them set their goals for the future and make plans to reach those goals. Drug education is a strong component and incorporates eight specific drug education seminars each year.

The Adolescent Social Action Program—The ASAP program utilizes volunteer, high-risk Hispanic and American Indian youths in grades six through ten who have been identified as nonusers of alcohol and other drugs. The primary emphasis of the program is to prepare youth, through experiential learning, for active involvement in community prevention activities and mobilization. Assisted by college students, teams of seven students visit hospital and detention center clients to interview them about their life experiences related to their use of drugs and alcohol. Participants and their parents receive an orientation before the visits, and the school curriculum is designed to allow the students to integrate their experiences. College students are trained by college faculty to help the youth.

REACH (Outdoor Adventure Club)—The Outdoor Adventure Club was organized as an alternative program to drug education for youth aged seven and up. Club members assemble every other week at LaFollette Tennessee Housing Authority for meetings that feature educational themes promoting the group's basic goal: "Get High the Natural Way!" Upon joining, each member signs an agreement with the club's counselors to support the group's goal. Activities stress positive addictions such as healthy bodies, minds and attitudes. Young people have an opportunity to maintain national and state parks through volunteer services. Counselors form relationships with the youth and encourage them to make positive decisions in their choices about drugs, school and friends.

Positive Option Program—This program was established ten years ago in Charlotte, North Carolina, to develop a mandatory educational series for students who violate school policy on alcohol and other drugs. The program allows both the student and the family to work together to seek positive alternatives to those forces that lead to alcohol and other drug use. The program consists of two-hour sessions in the evenings. Sessions attempt to raise the awareness about the dangers of alcohol and drug use, empower parents through resiliency building lessons and skills development, improve communication and decision making for both students and parents, and provide appropriate referrals for follow-up training and counseling.

San Antonio Fighting Back—This is a comprehensive drug prevention program of the United Way of San Antonio and the Robert Wood Johnson Foundation of Tennessee. The goal of the program is to establish a continuum of care to effectively address alcohol and other drug abuse through comprehensive prevention, intervention, treatment, and relapse prevention. Fighting Back is a collaboration and partnership with the community and is facilitated by a team of Community Coordinators and Neighborhood Networkers.

Boston Violence Prevention Program—The objectives of this program include: training youth agency personnel how to teach adolescents about the risks of violence and the measures youth can take to avoid being drawn into fights; meeting the psychological needs of adolescents who have been victims of violence; and using community involvement and the mass media to create a new community ethos in support of violence prevention. Because of a broad community education campaign, the program now encompasses all 12 of Boston's neighborhoods. In the first year, a mass media campaign was designed to raise public awareness of adolescent violence. The campaign featured public service announcements on the role of peer pressure and the responsibility of friends to help defuse conflict situations. Recently the project launched several experiments, including peer leadership training and summer camps.

HOSTS (Help One Student to Succeed)—The program was founded in 1971 and currently serves over 30,000 children on over 400 campuses nationwide. The program is successful because it breaks the cycle of student failure, accelerates learning and provides students with attention, love and personal caring to restore their confidence and enthusiasm for learning. Not a curriculum, HOSTS is an instructional strategy tailored to meet each school's goals, philosophies and state objectives. It is a structured mentoring and tutoring program in language arts, and is designed to reinforce lessons provided by the classroom teacher and reduce their workload. The program matches at-risk students with business and community volunteer mentors who work to strengthen students' reading, writing, vocabulary development and study skills. Volunteers are continuously recruited from civic clubs and community organizations, because each student in the program requires at least one volunteer mentor.

Lapham Park Association—The Lapham Park Association Center serves as an alternative educational program for troubled youth. It was designed to work toward changing the negative behavior patterns of those who were deemed "challenging" because of incidents that had resulted in referral to the central office. Students are sent to Lapham Park for violent behavior or weapon possession. The mission of the center is to provide students with many varied and positive school experiences in a caring and nurturing environment that is conducive to personal well-being. The goal is to provide students with an individually guided academic and counseling program aimed at improving behavior and increasing academic success.

Similar alternative placements are found throughout the United States and are funded from the Department of Public Instruction's

At-Risk Funds (69, line item in the budget manual). Each alternative school has specific procedures and guidelines for students. The most important factor is having teachers serving these students who sincerely want to do the job. In Haywood County Schools (North Carolina), teachers were selected by application only and then interviewed. Thus, teachers were selected based upon their interest in at-risk youth.

Problems of children with violent tendencies are extending from our streets into our schools at an alarming rate. Not only must America's educational institutions address these serious concerns, but schools are also forced to deal with other problems, including suicide, child abuse and lack of discipline. The days when student-related school problems consisted of a few playground squabbles and some kids playing hooky are long gone. School attendance and student discipline continue to be major concerns, but they are now part of a long list of issues that must be addressed to assure safe and effective schools for the nation's elementary and secondary school students.

In Chapter Three, school prevention and intervention will be stressed. The chapter will include school programs that have been initiated for safety, assistance from law enforcement, effective practices, and interagency collaboration. The magnitude of school crime and violence affecting both students and teachers can no longer be ignored. This critical issue has come to the forefront of public concern, but a long-term solution will require educators to work with parents, law enforcement officials and the community in implementing strategies of prevention and intervention to alleviate violence in our nation's schools.

CHAPTER THREE

School Prevention and Intervention

Recent schoolyard shootings include the following:

- February 2, 1996: In Moses Lake, Washington, 14-year-old Barry Loukaitis killed his teacher and two students, and wounded another.
- February 19, 1997: In Bethel, Alaska, 16-year-old Evan Ramsey opened fire, leaving the school principal and one student dead, and two wounded.
- October 1, 1997: In Pearl, Mississippi, 16-year-old Luke Woodham killed his mother and two classmates, and wounded seven others—and then claimed demon influence.
- December 1, 1997: In West Paducah, Kentucky, 14-year-old Michael Carneal brutally killed three students and wounded five others.
- December 15, 1997: In Stamps, Arkansas, 14-year-old Joseph Todd killed two fellow students.
- March 24, 1998: In Jonesboro, Arkansas, 13-year-old Mitchell Johnson and 11-year-old Andrew Golden ambushed their school, killing five with handguns and rifles.
- April 24, 1998: In Edinboro, Pennsylvania, 14-year-old Andrew

Wurst attacked people at his school dance, killing a science teacher with a handgun and wounding three others.

- April 28, 1998: In Pomona, California, a 14-year-old boy killed two students playing basketball at an elementary school.
- May 19, 1998: In Springfield, Oregon, 15-year-old Kip Kinkel killed both his parents at home and then two fellow students in the high school cafeteria, and wounded 19 others.

Making Schools Safe

There are two types of school administrators: those who have faced a crisis and those who are about to. In an ideal world, one would like to prevent all school violence and ensure a safe and orderly learning environment for all children. The reality is that so many things are out of the administrator's control that a safe and orderly learning atmosphere is virtually impossible. To attempt to predict every potentially dangerous situation involving a student, a staff member or an intruder who comes onto the campus is unrealistic. However, armed with the knowledge that violence can happen on a school campus, the administrator can do several things to prepare for a crisis and avoid successive crises.

No greater challenge exists today than creating safe schools. Restoring our schools to tranquil and safe places of learning requires a major strategic plan with commitment from all stakeholders. School safety should be placed at the top of all educational agendas. Without safe schools, teachers cannot teach and students cannot learn.

Developing district and school safety plans should be a requirement in each education agency. Developing safety plans is a critical part of good school planning and intervention. Every child that stays out of school is afraid to go to school—it's very sad that our children must be afraid to enter the schoolhouse doors. This sad fact is a national tragedy.

Administrators have a variety of strategies that can make schools safe. However, before implementing these strategies, support must be given by the superintendent and board of education.

In 1997, North Carolina passed the Safe Schools Act, which requires each school and district to submit a Safe Schools Plan. Each plan has to be local, and state approved. Revisions of the Safe Schools Plan must be reviewed and revised annually and the principal's bonus pay is tied to the plan. In Haywood County (Waynesville, North Carolina), the superintendent developed a checklist for safe schools. He visits each principal and checks on how well they have prepared their schools for safety and intervention strategies.

The Superintendent's Checklist involves the school principal documenting the following:

1. Student code of conduct and designed consequences for violating the code.

2. Role and responsibilities of all school personnel in maintaining a safe and orderly learning environment.

3. Procedures for identifying and serving the needs of students at risk of academic failure or of engaging in disorderly or disruptive behavior.

4. Mechanics for assessing the needs of the disruptive and disorderly students.

5. Measurable objectives for improving school safety and order.

6. Professional development clearly matched to the objectives for improving school safety and order.

7. Plans to work with local law enforcement and court officials to ensure safety.

8. A clear and detailed statement of the planned use of federal, state and local funds allocated for at-risk students, alternative schools, or both.

9. Methods of communicating the plan with the internal and external school community.

10. Emergencies (riots, assaults with deadly weapons, so on).

11. Safety of facility.

12. The development of an awareness program for school safety. Items may include parent meetings, a handbook, so on.

13. Establishing ongoing training for school personnel in all aspects of school safety. This training should occur at least biannually as per Board Policy A-31, Safe and Orderly Schools.

The superintendent has a conference with each principal to discuss documentation and evidence to fulfill the survey. It is the principal's responsibility to keep documentation on a yearly basis.

Safe school planning is not limited to special restraints or a specific set of guidelines. A Safe School Plan is a function of community wills, priorities and interests. To ensure that safe plans are successful, it is essential that partnerships are developed and priorities and interests prioritized. Crucial players include students, educators, parents, law enforcement officers, judges, recreation program directors, prosecutors, juvenile court supervisors, truant officers, mental health leaders, and other youth serving professionals.

A safe school is where teachers can teach and students can learn in a welcoming environment, free of fear and intimidation. It is an educational setting where the climate promotes a spirit of acceptance and care for every child; where behavior expectations are clearly communicated, consistently enforced, and fairly applied. Now, how do we make our schools safe?

Safety must be an important part of all educational units. This must be a top priority from the school board and the superintendent. Support must be gained from the administrators, faculty, staff, parents, students, and community. We hear constantly, "Those shootings could never happen at East High School, our community is too small." Bethel, Alaska; West Paducah, Kentucky; and Springfield, Oregon, probably all felt the same, that their schools and communities were safe. Look what happened…. No school or community is safe from the influx of violence and anger, both from students and intruders.

School administrators must:

1. Establish clear behavior standards.
2. Provide adequate adult presence and supervision.
3. Enforce the rules fairly and consistently.
4. Supervise closely and sanction offenders consistently.
5. Cultivate parental support.
6. Control campus access.
7. Create partnerships with outside agencies.
8. Believe they can make schools safe.

A comprehensive approach to school safety requires that school administrators and principals meet several challenges simultaneously. These challenges include:

1. Assessing the school's security needs.
2. Monitoring the school facility to ensure it is a clean, safe environment.
3. Implementing policies that support and reward positive social behavior.

4. Implementing schoolwide education and training on safety and avoiding violence.

5. Providing counseling and social services to students.

Physical Plant

A school's physical plant influences where crime will occur. Schools can be designed to limit access of unauthorized persons, increase the ability of school staff to visually supervise all areas of the school facility, and reduce crowding. Schools should be built with security in mind, but existing schools can make changes to their buildings to ensure safety. Installing adequate lighting and break-proof door and window locks, minimizing private storage areas, and eliminating removable ceiling panels are important safety measures all schools can adopt. The key to making the school environment safer is to use space constructively without creating a restrictive environment.

A professional school safety assessment is a good way to figure out just where the school stands, and what security weaknesses should be addressed. These assessment teams are available through each state's department of public instruction; private agencies are also prevalent.

Wolfgang Halbig, director of school security for the Seminole County (Florida) Schools decided to use an innovative approach to assessing school safety. He met with the school superintendent and sheriff's department and they decided to send undercover officers into the three schools for five months. This idea came from the corporate world, which employs professional shoppers to judge the performance of their employees when they are least expecting it. Two officers were selected to go undercover. Their first step was to immerse themselves in the teenage culture, hanging out at malls, and getting a feel for what it was like to be a teenager in Seminole County.

The officers were asked to look for the following:

1. How did the teachers respond to problems?
2. How extensive was gang involvement?
3. Who were the bullies? Was there extortion?
4. How well were teachers, administrators and SROs (school resource officers) doing their jobs?

At the conclusion of the five-month study, there were 42 arrests, which included drug-dealing students and parents. The arrests were only a small part of the benefits reaped at the two high schools in which undercover officers worked.

A good insight was gained into the problems facing schools today, and where improvement needed to be made.

The officers observed that first and foremost, students knew when and on a daily basis where the school's security priorities were. Students knew what sections of the schools were monitored and where the school resource officers spent their time. Officers and teachers need to rotate and randomize their schedules to avoid predictability. School resource officers need to be visible and in the hallways. The same is true for teachers and administrators. In Seminole County, neither teachers, administrators nor school resource officers were seen nearly as much as expected.

Another finding was that cafeterias were too crowded and students had to wait in line too long. The waiting and crowdedness created conflict and irritation among the students. The result was more fighting and assaults.

A very important observation was that high schools were too large. A revisiting of attendance zones was suggested.

It also helped to identify the major players in the school: which students controlled the hallways; who were the biggest drug dealers.

To make the school facility safe, 13 other acts of intervention were necessary:

1. To remove shrubbery that interferes with natural surveillance.
2. To provide supervision in heavy traffic areas.
3. To provide strategically located public telephones with dial-free connections to emergency services.
4. To relocate safe activities near typical trouble spots. A good example would be locating the teacher workstation near a corridor where problems occur.
5. To eliminate obstacles such as trash cans and architectural barriers that block or impede traffic flow as well as supervision and surveillance.
6. To use parabolic or convex mirrors in stairwells and locations that require continued supervision.
7. To be sure each classroom can communicate with the office. If buildings do not have intercom systems on which calls can be made to the office, the teachers should be provided with cell phones or a centrally located telephone.

8. To replace double-entry restroom doors with an open zigzag design to better monitor behavior in restroom areas. Automatic flush valves and automatic water faucets could be installed to reduce vandalism and control water consumption.

9. To remove posters from all windows. Posters and construction paper covering windows block supervision. Windows should be left clear so proper supervision can take place.

10. A lot of options exist for access control and property identification and supervision; for example, electromagnetic door locking systems. Proper control technology such as microdot systems and surveillance cameras for difficult to supervise public areas and other high-tech strategies may be appropriate.

11. Certain crime prevention policies have become popular in schools. Those preventive techniques might include: allowing only clear bookbags on campus or banning bookbags, eliminating lockers, establishing a coat check area for oversized articles of clothing capable of shielding weapons, or providing students with two sets of books, one for home and one for school, to eliminate the need for bookbags and school lockers. The purchase of two sets of textbooks is a very expensive proposition. At Waynesville Middle School (North Carolina), the PTO assisted with the purchase of extra books. The school eliminated all bookbags and school lockers. This action was prompted by a student at the school making a tennis ball bomb.

12. Several schools throughout the nation have hired security guards. Fees charged to students for parking privileges pay them. The guards check the parking lot throughout the day. They are stationed at the entrance to the campus and each person must sign in upon entering the campus grounds. This works very well because there is only one entrance and exit to the campus.

13. To conduct an annual review.

Safe Schools Plan

We have briefly discussed a safe school plan and the need for all stakeholders to feel ownership. A school level safety plan should be developed for each school. These plans will benefit from the collaboration of parents, students, educators, law enforcers, the courts, probation and social service personnel and religious, corporate and other community leaders who represent the racial and ethnic balance of the community. Safe school planning requires vigorous, ongoing interagency support. Community and corporate partnerships should not focus merely on security and supervision but also on education. Plans should be annually updated and broadly disseminated to students, parents and staff.

Specific items to be considered when creating a safe schools plan are:

1. To conduct a site assessment. You might consider calling the state department of public instruction to ask for an assistance team which would come to your school or educational unit and provide an on-site assessment. A lot of professional organizations also provide this service for a fee. The school needs to be assessed in terms of violent incidents. Daily walk-through inspections will provide the principal with items that can and need to be changed to promote a safe learning environment. Determine where you want the school to be, then develop a plan for getting to that point.

2. Collect data. What's happening in the community? Look at your school's security and safety policies and think about whether they will help you supervise your students. Administrators can search lockers; this is very controversial. You need to place in the student handbook or the code of conduct that lockers may and can be searched on regular intervals.

3. Send a copy of the site plan to the law enforcement officials because if a violent incident occurs they need to know how to respond to the site. Current floor plans, which include room numbers, teacher names, electrical sites, prove to be very useful to both administrators and law enforcement officers.

4. Analyze school crime reports. Knowing the safety concerns of the staff and students helps you deal with them. Talk with law enforcement to identify patterns and types of student violence problems. Also, review the school's media file; this will give insight into areas that should be addressed.

5. Community linkages are important. Urban schools have a bigger problem with this issue because people move more often in those districts, which makes forming relationships difficult. Because of the frequent moves of these children and families they do not have the opportunity to bond with peers and community.

6. Be culturally sensitive. Schools have to acknowledge the various cultural differences that students bring to school. If you will recall, on the checklist for students with tendencies toward violent

behavior (Chapter Two), hate groups and lack of tolerance for other races was an identifying trait of students who are likely to become violent.

7. Involve other agencies. Involve the juvenile justice department and invite the presiding judge to be on the school safety committee. In Orange County, California, a judge passed an order stating that the Justice Department can share information on minors with schools. Kentucky parents or guardians must notify the school if their child is arrested. In North Carolina, students entering a school for the first time must produce a signed notarized document stating that they have never been arrested for a felony.

A safe schools plan is a continuing, broad-based, comprehensive and systematic process to create and maintain a safe, secure and welcoming school climate, free of drugs, violence and fear; a climate which promotes the success and development of all children, and those professionals who serve them.

Among the components of an effective school safety plan are procedures for drug prevention, student leadership, parent participation, school security, community outreach and nuisance abatement.

Included in the safe school plan should be specific policies and guidelines for student behavior. These guidelines are typically called a code of conduct for students and are included in student and parent handbooks. More lives have been saved than lost by enforcing the standards of conduct on student speech, dress, verbalization of hate, weapons, search and seizure, discrimination, and other areas. Policies on all of these matters not only must be clearly communicated to students and their parents but also enforced fairly through disciplinary action consistently and equally applied. Policies and procedures to prevent violence are useless if they are not clearly publicized to students and followed and consistently enforced by teachers and administrators.

Crisis Plan

Crises occur whether we plan for them or not, and it is unlikely that any school will escape the necessity of responding to a significant crisis. However, because crises are usually unanticipated, crisis planning frequently gets lost in the day to day routine of operating a school.

A crisis can be defined as a sudden, generally unanticipated event that profoundly and negatively affects a significant segment of the school population and often involves serious injury or death.

Although experience has taught us we lack control over such events, we can prevent unnecessary turmoil. Planned schoolwide crisis management can significantly reduce disruption during times of high stress and can prevent catastrophic events from escalating into chaos. In situations affecting a smaller number of students and staff, or those in which the school serves primarily as a back-up to law enforcement, a structured response by a trained team or staff members can minimize damage and facilitate the return to a normal daily routine.

Any death or significant trauma to a student or staff member affects members of the school and community; however, most of these are essentially private griefs. In these cases, classroom attention, grief counseling and other routine support services offered by the school will suffice. From the administrator's point of view, these events do not constitute a crisis.

A crisis in one school setting may not be considered a crisis in another school setting.

In times of crisis, administrators will want to disrupt the school routine as little as possible to effectively control the situation. Developing a crisis management process is a significant step in making our schools safe.

Establishing a Crisis Plan

It is extremely important that the school staff and administrators make advance plans for crisis situations. A school that is prepared before a crisis occurs will be much more likely to deal with students and staff effectively.

The following steps should prove helpful in developing a crisis management plan:

1. Decide who will be in charge during the crisis.
2. Select your crisis response team.
3. Develop clear and consistent policies and procedures.
4. Provide training for the crisis response team.
5. Establish a police liaison.
6. Establish a media liaison and identify suitable facilities where reporters can work and news conferences can be held.

7. Establish a working relationship with community health agencies and other resource groups.

8. Establish phone trees.

9. Plan to make space available for community meetings and for outside service providers involved in crisis management.

10. Develop necessary forms and information sheets.

11. Develop a plan for emergency coverage of classes.

12. Establish a code to alert staff.

13. Develop a collection of readings.

14. Have the school attorney review crisis response procedures and forms.

15. Hold a practice crisis alert session.

16. Hold an annual workshop or in-service course on general crisis intervention.

A comprehensive crisis plan for dealing with situations should include:

- A crisis response team with clearly defined duties.
- A plan for evacuating the school.
- A plan for coordinating with and notifying police, elected officials, government agencies, and proper authorities.
- A plan for notifying parents quickly.
- A media/communications strategy.
- Counselors available to deal with students in the aftermath of a traumatic event.

Zero Tolerance Policies

Three-quarters or more of all schools reported having zero tolerance policies for various student offenses. A zero tolerance policy can be defined as one in which a school or district mandates predetermined consequences or punishments for specific offenses. About 90 percent of schools reported zero tolerance for threats, weapons and firearms. Eighty-seven percent had zero tolerance for drugs and alcohol. Seventy-nine percent had zero tolerance for violence and tobacco.

Threats/Threatening Situation, Recommendations

In Memphis City School District, principals and teachers were cracking down on students who made threats. They were suspending students and telling them to never come back. Now the district has developed a policy to provide a consistent model for its school personnel to follow. Schools need to develop a fair and consistent procedure when dealing with students who make threats to others.

Haywood County Schools (Waynesville, North Carolina) was one of the first systems in the United States to develop specific guidelines for threats. They define a threat as "any communication, written, verbal or otherwise, that implies bodily harm to self or others or to destruction of property." Every threat or threatening situation is handled immediately by school administrators. Each school developed a plan to secure buildings for the purpose of protecting students and staff from potentially harmful persons and events.

Every staff member, who hears or learns of a threat against property or persons, is required to complete a threat incident report. This form is taken immediately to the principal's office along with the person responsible for making the threat.

The principal (or their designee) talks with the parties involved. Action taken may include a warning, a parent conference, in-school or out-of-school suspension, counseling referral or law enforcement intervention. If law enforcement is called, the principal will immediately fax the completed copy of the threat form to the superintendent.

Parents of a student responsible for making the threat will be notified immediately by the principal. If the threat is against another student, that student's parents are notified as deemed appropriate by the principal.

The principal may require persons involved to speak with a certified mental health counselor before returning to school. Schools ask parents to sign a release form for permission for information to be shared between the school and the mental health authorities. Parents are responsible for the cost of the evaluation. The student is not allowed to return to school until the mental health counselor notifies the school in writing that the student has been evaluated and will follow through with any treatment recommendation. As part of the mental health plan, the school and the agency may request a multidisciplinary meeting. The meeting includes a representative from the school principal, counselor, mental health representative, parent, student, and others as deemed appropriate. If the child fails to follow through with treatment or recommendations, the school will be notified. In the event the child withdraws from recommended treatment without permission of the mental health experts, the principal may exercise any option necessary including out-of-school suspension. Upon the student's return to school, the counselor will have contact with them to monitor their stability. A law enforcement or juvenile services officer may visit the home to advise parents and family members of the legal ramifications of threatening conduct and to assess the availability of weapons to the student. Law enforcement will contact juvenile authorities on a needs basis.

Any student that makes a threat is required to have a parent conference with the principal before they return to campus.

All faculty and staff are required to familiarize themselves with the following profile of a student who may pose a threat to others. This list was obtained from the National School Safety Center. It should be noted that no profile could be all-inclusive. All faculty and staff should therefore be alert to other unusual or aberrant behavior. The student:

- Has tantrums and uncontrollable angry outbursts.
- Characteristically resorts to name calling, cursing or abusive language.
- Habitually makes violent threats when angry.
- Has previously brought a weapon to school.
- Has a background of serious disciplinary problems.
- Has a background of drug, alcohol or other substance abuse or dependency.
- Has few or no close friends.
- Has no "mother" figure in the home.
- Is preoccupied with weapons, explosives or incendiary devices.
- Displays cruelty to animals.
- Has witnessed or been the victim of neglect or abuse in the home.
- Bullies or intimidates peers or younger children.
- Tends to blame others for difficulties and problems he causes.
- Consistently prefers TV shows, reading materials, movies or music expressing violent themes, rituals and abuse.
- Reflects anger, frustration and the dark side of life in school writing projects.

- Is involved with a gang or an antisocial group on the fringe of peer acceptance.
- Is often depressed or has attempted suicide.

Being familiar with the profile will enable all staff members to be proactive in terms of observing these students and changes if they occur. Any student in this category who fits this profile will be referred to the principal. In the absence of a threat, but if characteristics of the profile are observed, parents will be notified. If needed, the school counselor will notify the mental health counselor as appropriate.

A folder for documentation will be generated at the site for the identified students. If the student transfers within the education unit, all information will be forwarded to the receiving school. The principal is responsible for transferring this folder to the appropriate principal.(Confidentiality is similar to that in juvenile record cases.)

Each principal will serve as the contact person to receive information from the community about threatening incidents. Each principal and central office person is provided with a beeper so they may be contacted if a need arises.

If a report of a serious threatening situation occurs after school hours, the principal will take any of the following steps depending on the severity of the situation:

- Contact parents and require a conference before the next school day.
- Call law enforcement officials.
- Take additional steps as necessary to ascertain the seriousness of the threat and to protect students, staff, and property.

All staff are notified immediately when a student previously removed from campus for a threatening incident returns without authorization. If students return illegally, they will be charged with trespassing by the law officers, or if students are near the facility but not legally on school grounds, officers will be called. When the student is legally allowed back on school grounds, the staff will be notified.

Signs are placed at each entrance stating that all threats are taken seriously.

This is the second year of implementation for the threat and threatening situation policy in Haywood County. The plan was created jointly by principals, central office, parents, students, board of education members, law enforcement officers, mental health counselors and a psychologist. The committee meets annually to review the policy and to make revisions.

During the second year of implementation, threat incidents were reduced by 50 percent.

There is always a concern about the school's liability. While school districts and officials generally have immunity from suits under state law, a critical issue that always will need to be confronted is the foreseeability of the kinds of disasters and tragedies we have witnessed in recent years. In other words, was the school on notice, or was a particular teacher on notice, that this was an especially dangerous student who had made specific threats or shown clear indications that he would commit a violent act against his fellow students. Policies and procedures for threats or threatening incidents can prove to be crucial in identifying students and taking extra precautions. While the standard of liability is the deliberate indifference of an administrator when put on notice of the violation of a code of conduct, a Maryland court held that school personnel had a heightened duty to act upon the knowledge of a student's threat of suicide, based on the school's inherent duty to protect students from harm.

School Resource Officers

President Clinton's reaction to the recent shootings was to request that then Attorney General Janet Reno and Education Secretary Richard W. Riley find ways for the federal government to provide more police officers in the schools. The President also endorsed Representative James H. Maloney's bill to increase the number of law officers available to deal with crime prevention and school delinquency problems.

The concept of the school resource officer was first initiated in Flint, Michigan, in the early 1950s. Since that time, a number of agencies have had school resource officers, or SROs. However, the first formalized program was created in Florida.

The Florida Legislature mandated that there be SROs statewide in all middle and high schools. Now, there are a number of police officers throughout the nation that have been trained as SROs using the Florida model.

The goal of long-term school resource officers is to reduce drug-related and violent crimes committed by juveniles in middle and high schools. The officer will provide law-related education and safety programs, one on one interaction, conflict resolution and peer mediation for the students.

Project Guidelines:

1. Deliver drug and safety education programs in the classroom when schedules permit.

2. Establish one on one interaction between SRO and students.

3. Establish trust between students and SRO.

4. Establish outlets for students to participate in peer mediation and conflict resolution to enable them to arrive at peaceful solutions to problems.

5. Provide deterrence to drugs and violent behavior by physical presence and counseling.

6. Involve known offenders in the program in an attempt to change attitudes regarding illegal and violent activities.

7. Receive daily reports from school principal or their designee about suspensions, in-school isolation, and other major disciplinary actions and conduct follow-ups with involved parties.

8. Receive reports from juvenile officer concerning suspected activity or juvenile arrests involving juveniles at the officer's assigned school.

9. Confer with teachers to measure project effectiveness and to help identify problems with students or the program.

10. Perform follow-ups with students, parents or guardians as to juvenile behavior. Advise parents or guardians of potential problems with children based on the SRO's observation on a daily basis.

11. Assist in outside investigations involving juveniles at SRO's assigned school, or handle investigation if appropriate.

12. Keep accurate records of problems and cases and prepare reports for juvenile intake.

13. SROs should establish themselves as a credible source of trust and knowledge and encourage participation by students.

14. Assist with truants by helping eliminate reasons not to attend school.

It is interesting to note that there does not exist a job description or a salary schedule for school resource officers. It is quite common for the school principal, central office and the law enforcement agency to sit down together and develop their own job description and a salary schedule. Some schools contract with SROs for an hourly rate and other units use teacher salary schedules to compensate the officer.

The following is a job description for an SRO, which has been cut and pasted from several states and agencies. The SRO shall:

1. Abide by school board policies and shall consult with and coordinate activities through the school principal but shall remain fully responsive to the chain of command of the law enforcement in all matters relating to employment and supervision.

2. Develop expertise in presenting various subjects particularly in meeting federal and state mandates in drug abuse prevention education and shall provide these presentations at the request of the school personnel in accordance with the established curriculum.

3. Encourage individual and small group discussions about law enforcement related matters with students, faculty and parents.

4. Refrain completely from functioning in school disciplinary infractions that do not constitute violations of the law.

5. Attend meetings of parents and faculty to solicit their support and understanding of the School Resource Officer program and to promote awareness of law enforcement functions.

6. Serve as a member of the Student Services Committee and shall be familiar with all community agencies which offer assistance to youths and their families such as mental health clinics and drug treatment centers and make referrals when appropriate.

7. Confer with the principal to develop plans and strategies to prevent or minimize dangerous situations on or near the campus involving students at school-related activities.

8. As determined by the principal, perform duties regularly assigned to other school personnel such as lunchroom or hall duty. Nothing herein is intended to preclude the SRO from being available in areas where interaction with students is expected.

9. Abide by school board policy and applicable laws concerning interviews should it be necessary to conduct formal law enforcement interviews with students or staff on property or at school functions under the jurisdiction of the school board.

10. Take law enforcement action as necessary and notify the principal of the school as soon as possible; whenever practicable advise the principal before requesting additional enforcement assistance on campus and undertake all additional law enforcement responsibilities at the principal's discretion.

11. Give assistance to officers in accordance with the duties of SROs whenever necessary.

12. In order to assure the peaceful operation of school-related programs, participate in or attend school functions.

13. Reaffirm their roles as law enforcement officers by wearing their uniforms, unless doing so would be inappropriate for scheduled school activities. The uniform shall also be worn at events where it will enhance the image of the officers and their ability to perform their duties.

14. Coordinate with the principal and be responsible for law enforcement and security activity at extracurricular events as determined by the principal.

15. Attend workshops and in-service courses concerning job responsibilities.

Requirements

Job requirements vary from state to state. However, the majority concurred that the following were required:

1. Two-year college degree.
2. Three to four years in law enforcement as a sworn officer.
3. Certified as a law enforcement agent within the state in which they are working.
4. Would prefer experience as a School Resource Officer and currently employed full time in a law enforcement capacity.

Selecting an SRO

The process for selecting an SRO should be multistaged. There should be a requirement for some minimum amount of time on the street. While a college degree does not ensure success, an individual who posseses such a qualification will be more easily accepted by school administrators and staff. The individual selected should represent the department in an exemplary fashion and show a demonstrated interest in working with young people. One of the final steps in the screening should include an interview by the principal, school improvement team and the police chief or sheriff.

Training

The curriculum that has been adopted from Florida is a 40-hour, one-week course. The topics include Community Resource and Resource

Development, Exceptional Children and Dysfunctional Families, and Counseling Techniques. Other items include:

- Define the SRO concept and apply this to the school in which they are assigned.
- Define the dual objectives of prevention and enforcement as it applies to the SRO.
- Identify the functions of the SRO within the law enforcement agency.
- Identify the role of the SRO in the educational community.
- Apply juvenile law and public school law to the specific job duties.
- Identify the various classifications of those students involved in the Exceptional Children's Program and sensitize the SRO to each classification.
- Discuss the problems of adolescent suicide, identify the warning signs associated with "at-risk" students and recommend the appropriate steps which need to be taken in handling these students.
- Identify effective instructional strategies to assist students with implementing law related educational programs with a delinquency prevention impact.
- Discuss the development of relationships necessary to function as an SRO, including relationships with students, parents and faculty.
- How to teach an instructional class at the middle or high school level.
- Discuss the trends of school violence and the influence of gangs, and drugs in the school setting.

Operating an SRO Program

The school to which an SRO is assigned becomes that officer's zone, or patrol area. The SRO is expected to:

- Be at the school each day when school is open.
- Attend all school functions including dances, athletic events, and PTA meetings.
- Be available to attend conferences and meetings.

The SRO should have an assigned office that can be locked to prevent intrusion and is equipped with a telephone. A computer linked to the law enforcement agency will save hours of paper work and travel off campus. The SRO is responsible for processing individuals arrested on school grounds unless the department has a different policy.

Funding of an SRO

Most states receive code 69 or at-risk funds which can be used to totally fund the SRO's position. Other educational systems pay for the positions through local funds. In North Carolina, several SROs have been funded through the Governor's Crime Commission Grant—this pays for the position for two years which would allow sufficient time to search for other sources of revenue. A very common source of funding is a 50/50 split. The school system pays 50 percent of the officer's salary and benefits and the law enforcement agency pays the other 50 percent. Transportation can also take a number of forms—for example, one officer in Fayetteville, North Carolina, arrives at school in a gold Cadillac that was seized from a drug dealer. The vehicle was outfitted with blue lights and sirens and has been used as a regular squad car. When law enforcement receives a new vehicle they sometimes assign an older vehicle to the SRO. The presence of a police car on campus has a direct impact on student and parent behavior.

The Promise of an SRO Program

An SRO program is a promising strategy because it enables communities and schools to address school violence with both prevention and intervention techniques. Having an SRO on a school campus can prevent problems from happening. When problems do arise, the SROs can intervene quickly to address them. The end result is that the school is safer and more secure for students, teachers, and staff. The entire community benefits as well because learning is more likely to take place in such an environment.

How to Deal with Gangs

Despite their differences, all gangs have elements in common. They offer kids status, acceptance, and self-esteem they haven't found elsewhere. In poorer communities, a breakdown of family and community structures may leave kids particularly susceptible to gang recruitment.

However, gangs also form in affluent areas among kids who feel alien-ated from friends and family.

Gang members proudly announce their membership through distinctive dress and behaviors. Bandannas and shoelaces of specific colors, jewelry, tattoos, jargon, and hand gestures all indicate gang affiliation. Many members carry weapons, both for potential use and to bolster their image. Members mark their territory with spray-painted graffiti or gang symbols. Turf lines are usually drawn in neigh-borhoods and fought over, but gang rivalries are also fought out in the schools.

School districts alone can't solve the problems of gangs; no single agency can. There has to be cooperation among schools, criminal jus-tice agencies and community organizations. Los Angeles created an interagency gang task force to enable the various agencies working on the gang issue to discuss gang problems and possible solutions.

The Governor of Oregon established a gang task force at the state level. It includes state police, Portland city and school police, and the sheriffs' offices of counties serving the Portland metropolitan area.

A coordinated effort is more likely to be successful when trying to eliminate gangs. However, straight suppression and straight interven-tion just don't work. Gangs are orphan institutions that kids turn to if they aren't making it in the mainstream. The most successful programs focus on helping younger kids do better in school and providing older kids with training and jobs, thereby addressing conditions that give rise to gangs.

Administrators in the Beaverton School District, southwest of Portland, are all too aware of the threat of spreading gangs. As long as they follow the rules, they are allowed to attend school. The school dis-trict is doing its best to keep the gang presence from increasing, and nonstudent gang members who try to recruit students are told they are trespassing and ordered off school grounds. The local police then enforce the law.

A different tactic is used to block members from enrolling. By Ore-gon law, a student under 18 has no automatic right to attend school unless their parent or guardian resides within the district.

School personnel need up-to-date information about gang activi-ties and symbols. Updated awareness sessions need to be conducted on a regular basis by law enforcement, gang experts and administrators. Some school districts have police give gang awareness sessions before any gang activity has appeared.

Weapons

Have you seen these headlines in the news?

"St. Louis Student, 14 Stabbed at School"
"Parents vs. New Student Violence"
"Bill's Aim: Get Parents to Lock Up Guns"
"Guns: Bill Is Full of Loopholes, Powerless Against Black Market"
"District to Set Up Weapons Hot Line"
"Montgomery Suspends 3 Young Boys"
"Why Do Kids Bring Weapons to School?"
"Students Stabbed at Buena High School"
"Stabbing: Student Attacked at School"
"Youth Charged in Reseda High Killing"

Ridding the public schools of weapons cannot effectively be addressed in isolation from other directly related issues. Time and again the primary reason children bring weapons to school is for self-protection traveling to and from school. Violence is a problem at schools, but principally it is a community problem. Many schools are surrounded by a 360-degree perimeter of community crime. Consequently, the strategies developed in response to school safety needs must go beyond the schools. The presence of weapons at schools cannot be separated from other community safety concerns.

An effective weapons reduction strategy must be multidisciplinary, comprehensive, politically sensitive and practically relevant. Both districtwide consistency and a measure of local autonomy are needed. Developing a comprehensive and systemwide response to school safety is a complex and intricate task at best. There is no magic formula. However, there are a variety of strategies the school district can consider to minimize weapon problems. These strategies must begin at the elementary level.

- Use tips from students. Providing a hotline for reporting weapons and other criminal activity can encourage this. In a North Carolina school district, a hotline has been established through the local crisis center and volunteers have been thoroughly trained on how to deal with these issues.

- Have a school security officer on campus. The person needs to be trained in law enforcement and working with young people.
- Locker searches. Schools own the lockers and therefore are entitled to search them as frequently as they desire. School officials who conduct such searches should receive training regarding reasonable suspicion so they understand the parameters of a legal search. Some school districts have banned lockers and students are required to carry the items they need or leave such items in their homerooms.
- Zero tolerance. The possession or use of a weapon or dangerous instruments results in automatic expulsion from the school system in several states. In Providence, Rhode Island, a student caught with a weapon is automatically suspended for 60 days. Polk County, Florida, expelled a student for the remainder of the school year as well as the following year. Detroit, Michigan, expels a student permanently from the school district when they bring a weapon on campus. Expelling and suspending students are both temporary solutions to the problem of weapons on school campus. They are not long-term solutions to the larger community problem.
- Metal detectors. This is a very controversial strategy but more and more schools are obtaining them. The use of metal detectors sends a strong message to students and the community that there is a problem with weapons and we are serious about solving it. These items are very useful at athletic events and at the entrance to schools to screen students and visitors.

Dress Codes

Whether about gang attire, Nazi insignias, trench coats or obscene messages, the emphasis should not be on the content or point of view of the speech or expression, but on the threat to discipline and safety in the schools. Due to the unfortunate incidents in Arkansas, Kentucky, Oregon, Colorado and Georgia, courts are more likely to uphold a school's right to enforce a well-developed dress code; this was evidenced by an April 30, 1999, decision by a federal judge in Salt Lake City which upheld a decision to suspend a student for wearing what would seem to be a benign article of clothing—a shirt that said "vegan," a reference to vegetarians who do not eat animal products. He noted that gang attire has become particularly troubling since two students wore trench coats in the Colorado shootings.

Students and staff tend to behave the way they are allowed to dress. Establish a districtwide dress code policy that sets specific and unambiguous appearance standards for both students and staff. Gang attire should be prohibited, and dress code expectations should be consistently enforced. Contradictory policies and procedures and inconsistent enforcement by staff send mixed messages to students. School staff should serve as role models for students. Involve students and parents in developing appearance standards. Students and parents will support and preserve what they help to create.

School Uniforms

Three percent of all public schools require students to wear uniforms. About one fourth of these schools initiated the requirement prior to the 1994-95 school year, 40 percent initiated it between the 1994-95 and 1995-96 school years, and 34 percent initiated it in 1996-97.

Uniforms were more likely to be required in schools with a high percentage of students eligible for free or reduced lunches (11 percent in schools with 75 percent or more on free or reduced lunch eligibility) than schools in which less than 50 percent of students were eligible. Schools with 50 percent or more minority enrollment were also more likely to require student uniforms than with those with lower minority enrollment (13 percent, compared with 2 percent or less).

Long Beach, California, recently got its first report card on a precedent-setting experiment with mandatory uniforms for all students at public elementary and middle schools. Grade: an honor-roll performance.

Crime plunged at the system's 56 elementary and 14 middle schools. Fewer weapons and drugs were found. Vandalism dropped. Unexpected benefits: declining absenteeism and improving academic performance among some of the 58,500 students. School spokesman Dick Van Laan credits uniforms with "wonderful changes, far exceeding our hopes."

In return, students relinquished some freedom. No more wearing of gang colors. No more shorts or skirts leaving nothing to the imagination. No more oversized shirts or baggy pants hanging below pelvic bones, an ideal get-up for weapons concealment.

In 1994, Long Beach's board of education voted to become the first public school district to require uniforms. Across the country, a growing number of public schools are experimenting with both uniforms and dress codes.

Key provisions for requiring students to wear uniforms include:

- Making certain there is a high level of parental support before the decision to require them is made.
- Allowing each school to select its own uniforms that are affordable, easy to care for and widely available from many competitive sources.
- Working with community groups to provide uniform assistance to disadvantaged children.
- Taking positive steps to assure compliance.
- Monitoring the impact of uniforms.
- Communicating the impact.

The bottom line for any exemplary educational reform is to elevate standards of excellence for all students—not only in dress, but also in conduct and achievement. School uniforms have had a positive impact on all three.

Prohibit Hate Speech

This is a very difficult area in which to develop a policy, but if one is carefully created it can be justified by removing the unpleasantness that hate speech can cause. Research shows that the psychic injury resulting from hate speech can be a potentially disruptive effect to the order and operation of the school.

Enhance Multicultural Understanding and Tolerance

Polarization among student groups and the rise in gang activity indicate a need to develop educational programs that bring students together and focus on cultural cooperation and tolerance. Such measures can easily be incorporated into a good character education program.

Ban Forms of Nonphysical Intimidation

Hard looks, stares, "mad-dogging" and "mean-mugging" should be added as actionable offenses to the student code of conduct. Such threatening behavior should not be tolerated. Psychological intimidation can be as damaging as physical assaults.

Implement a Peer Counseling and Peer Mediation Program

Students represent some of the best agents for promoting and maintaining safety on school campuses. An effective peer-counseling program can head off many problems before they reach explosive levels. Students trained as peer counselors can serve as influential resources for nonviolent problem solving.

Screen New Employees

One key decision parents and communities make involves deciding who will teach, train, coach, counsel and lead their children. Keeping child molesters and pedophiles out of classrooms, schools and youth serving organizations is a major task. The desire to provide responsible parenting and thoughtful leadership in schools and other youth serving agencies should be enough reason to establish appropriate safeguards for keeping child molesters away from children. In addition, increasing litigation against school systems and childcare providers has created a financial reason to conduct appropriate background checks to protect the safety of children. Some school systems and youth service organizations have faced multimillion dollar lawsuits for their failure to appropriately screen, properly supervise or remove employees who may have presented a risk for children. Every school system should have clear policies and guidelines to weed out individuals with criminal backgrounds of misbehavior involving children. Any record screening program must consider the rights of privacy and due process as well as the right to a hearing when disqualification is involved. The screening program must also balance these rights against the rights of the children who will be served by the individual.

Effective Programs and Practices

Expand Alternative Placement Options for Troubled Youth

Students who have committed weapons violations and other serious disruptions should be removed from the mainstream educational setting and relocated to an in-school suspension program or alternative education site within the district where closer supervision and greater structure are provided.

Research tells us that a relatively small percentage of students account for most of the violent incidents at school. Providing special services to this group of adolescents is essential for increasing school safety. If a student continues to commit repeated acts of serious violence, the school administrators may be obligated to place this student in a separate educational setting to assure the safety of other students and staff. Separating violent and weapon-carrying students from the general student body sends the message that school administrators have acted appropriately to preserve school safety and allows the special needs of these students to be met effectively. Alternative programs are preferred to suspensions and expulsions because they avoid shifting violent students onto the streets with little supervision. Common features of effective alternative schools include strong administrators, dedicated and well-trained staff, needs-based assessment of each child, a low student-to-teacher ratio, and counseling for students and their parents.

An alternative learning program seeks to serve students whose needs are not met in the traditional school setting. Alternative education is based on the belief that there are many ways to become educated as well as many types of environments and structures within which education may occur. Such a program may be designed:

- To serve students at any level.
- For suspended or expelled students.
- For students whose learning styles are better served in an alternative program.
- To use multiple strategies including serving students in the standard classroom, or by providing individualized programs outside of standard classroom setting in a caring atmosphere in which students learn the skills necessary to redirect their lives.

Alternative learning programs may take the form of schools within schools or separate freestanding institutions. They may graduate students directly from their program or seek to return students to the traditional high school. They may exist within a single district or as a consortium of several districts operated through an intermediate school district. They may offer instructional services during nontraditional school hours as well as during traditional school hours.

Common types of alternative education include:

- Continuation schools which provide an option for dropouts, potential dropouts, pregnant students, and teenage parents. These are designed to be less competitive and to provide a more individualized approach to learning. Programs vary, but usually include individualized learning plans that accommodate support services, personal responsibility for attendance and progress, non-graded or continuous progress, and personal or social development experiences.
- Schools within schools represent an option developed to reduce large schools, in size and numbers, to more manageable and humane units. They may be large groups within one building, along the lines of the middle school concept, or a small number of students who need individualized instruction and special support services. The program is designed to enhance student achievement, teach responsible classroom behaviors, and motivate regular school attendance.

Components of Good Alternative Learning Programs

There are several components which must be addressed if alternative education is to meet the individual needs of troubled or disruptive students:

Active parent involvement should be encouraged. This can be accomplished through positive contacts with parents by school officials, through training sessions, group meetings, and school activities.

Students should be given opportunities to get involved in public service.

- The school should have a well-defined mission statement, which seeks to provide a therapeutic and academically challenging program for assigned students. For those students in continuation schools and schools within schools who have been severely disruptive or involved in criminal activity, one of the goals should be to equip them to return to the regular school program as soon as possible.

- All personnel within the school should promote a caring atmosphere evidenced by mutual respect, high expectations, and a sense of community.
- A low teacher-student ratio allows students and teachers to work together cooperatively and students to receive the individual attention they may need.
- A successful alternative school requires a highly trained and skilled staff that operates as a team.
- Alternative programs for disruptive students need the local educational unit's best teachers.
- Teachers need to want to be at the school; they should not be placed there because they have had problems at other schools. Alternative schools should not be a dumping ground for unwanted staff members.
- A full contingent of professional student support services should be available to all students. These services include: counseling, psychological, and social services that will address the social, behavioral, and emotional problems of designated students.
- The school should operate under a system of positive discipline.
- The school should provide each student with a relevant, high quality, and meaningful curriculum.
- The program should be designed to enhance the self-esteem of each student.
- The alternative program should maintain regular contact with teachers and administrators from the home school from which the student was referred until the student is returned to the home school.
- The school or local educational unit should address all due process procedures for students and their parents who may want to contest student assignments to alternative schools.
- In cases where the alternative program is serving disruptive students, the school should develop an individual plan for improving student behavior and dealing with the underlying reason for the student's referral to the alternative program. In addition, there should be regular and comprehensive evaluations of each

student's progress based on established measurable objectives for each student.
- Community volunteers should serve as tutors, mentors, and big brothers and sisters.

Schools throughout the nation have initiated strategies to provide safer environments for students and staff. Hopefully, these strategies are based on an assessed need, modified as required and evaluated to determine their impact.

There is not a single or simple answer to the problem of violence; consequently, its reduction will require a multifaceted, comprehensive, collaborative approach which brings all of the forces at a school's disposal to bear. It must be addressed through the disciplinary programs, school curriculum, teaching methods, physical security and school and societal cultures. Everyone must be involved and everyone must be responsible.

The following are descriptions of strategies that may be initiated based on a school's assessment and needs:

- Agreements—Students and staff learn to settle disputes through active listening, acceptance of others' viewpoints, cooperation and creative problem solving.
- Integrated Curriculum—Emphasizes violence prevention through the existing curriculum by development of self-assessment, communication, decision making, health advocacy and self-management.
- Conflict Resolution—Resolving disagreements nonviolently by working together in a mutually acceptable way.
- Problem Solving—Students learn to analyze difficult situations and brainstorm ways for dealing with them.
- Decision Making—Students analyze situations, and determine different ways for dealing with them and the consequences involved.
- Self-Esteem Enhancement—Refers to programs that emphasize character development, positive social interaction, active listening and value clarification.
- Social Skills—Training in social skills helps students to successfully interact with others. It includes maintaining self-control, building communication skills, forming friendships, resisting peer pressure, being appropriately assertive and forming good relationships with adults.

- Cultural Diversity—Refers to programs and activities designed to provide understanding and awareness of the various gender, racial, religious, ethnic, and other cultural groups that make up the United States.
- Prevention of Sexual Harassment—Programs and activities that seek to prevent sexual harassment through enhanced understanding of what it is and guidelines for dealing with its incidence.
- Danger Awareness—Accident prevention program intended to teach children that guns are not toys. Through lectures, skits, and films students are taught why and how to stay away from firearms and other dangerous situations and to alert an adult if they come across them.
- Psychological Services—Consultations with mental health professionals. May include referrals to and contractual and cooperative agreements with mental health professionals and agencies to provide psychiatric and psychological services to students and their families.
- Counseling—Educational or therapeutic sessions and seminars offered to individuals or groups. Include case management approach to helping students through the development of individualized educational plans.
- Family Therapist—Usually an individual trained in family therapy or social work to help individual families resolve their problems.
- Peer Mediation—Disputants sit down with a trained student mediator in a designated sequestered area. The student mediator explains the ground rules, and usually the disputants are able to talk through the problem, brainstorm their solution, and sign a written agreement.
- Peer Helper—A student who is having problems has the option of discussing them with another student who has been trained in peer helping.
- Teen Court—The use of legal processes by students to decide consequences (in lieu of traditional punishment) for those students who admit to violation of school safety policies. Participation is voluntary.
- Student-Led Organizations—Student organizations established to promote responsibility for a safe school environment (for instance, Students Against Violence Everywhere, Youth Crime Watch, and Students Against Drunk Drivers).

- Mentoring—An adult provides a positive, caring influence and standard of conduct for young people. Mentors provide counseling, tutoring, and spend quality time with students. Additionally, through the ongoing guidance of teachers, high school teachers serve as mentors to younger middle and elementary school students.
- Manhood Development—These types of programs provide guidance and support to young men in overcoming confusion and frustration that lead to choosing destructive alternatives. The programs center their activities on self-esteem enhancement, pride in one's cultural heritage, and guidance for youth as they move from one stage of life to another.
- Crisis Intervention—An action plan for dealing with crisis situations. This includes guidelines for responding, incident priorities, and various staff roles.
- Security—Refers to individuals who provide school security but are not members of a law enforcement agency or working under the auspices of a law enforcement agency.
- Metal Detector—A magnetometer that is used to screen individuals entering the school for metal objects. The hand-held models have become very popular and are used frequently at school sponsored events.
- Environmental Design—Refers to lighting, paint color, shrubbery, wall recesses and other architectural aspects of the school.
- Identification Badges—An identification system in which students and staff are issued a badge, preferably with a photograph, to be worn so that it is visible.
- Surveillance Equipment—Electronic security systems that are specifically designed for intrusion detection. These include alarms, closed-circuit television cameras, motion detectors, and photoelectric beams.
- Video Cameras—Video cameras are installed on buses to record students' actions. The cameras are housed in boxes that make it impossible to tell if they are recording or not.
- Electronic Communication—Refers to multichannel radios such as walkie-talkies, cellular telephones and other similar equipment.
- Magnetic Locks—Electronic locks that can be remotely opened by a school official.
- Reward Programs—Programs that pay cash for anonymous information on weapons or the perpetrators of campus crime.

Usually a tip hotline is provided and callers are given a code number to help them claim cash for the information given.

- Juvenile Advocacy Officer—Individuals who work to bring about a more cooperative effort between the schools and courts.
- Policies/Regulations—School policies and regulations are reflective of recent state and federal safe schools legislation. They have been publicized to students and the community and are consistently enforced.
- Parental Involvement—Strategies and activities that schools and districts employ to increase parental presence in the schools and help prevent violence at home.
- Home Visitation—Services are provided in the home either for an individual or the entire family. They are typically designed to meet the needs of parents for information, emotional support, stress management and other factors.
- Recreational—Programs that provide young people opportunities to spend time in a structured and purposeful environment during leisure time.
- Work Experience—Structured job experiences connect youth with supportive adults as they perform useful tasks and play positive roles in society.
- Community Service—Students are involved in community-based agencies to help themselves and others deal with social problems.
- Media Campaign—Information that draws the public's attention to an issue and helps to establish acceptable behavior. Some examples are public service announcements, educational videos, appearances on talk shows, posters, brochures and other print materials.

Integrated Curriculum

While it is now popular and recommendable to have stand-alone conflict resolution curricula, the stand-alone should be part of a comprehensible approach to safer schools and should not replace the teaching of conflict resolution as an integral part of the existing curriculum. The curriculum should include active listening, effective communications, cooperative problem solving, identifying facts and issues, decision making, identifying solutions, and discussing and reaching agreements. Certain curricular areas, such as healthful living education, social studies, language arts, and guidance, were originally designed to target violence.

School systems can acquire appropriate supplemental materials plan targeted staff development, and develop programs based on successful models. By integrating conflict resolution and mediation skills into the existing curriculum, students progressing from kindergarten to grade 12 can acquire the behaviors needed to respond nonviolently to conflict.

A healthful living curriculum should outline numerous specific goals for young people that are directed toward violence prevention. For example, at the high school level, the healthful living curriculum emphasizes accepting responsibility for one's own thoughts, feelings, and behaviors, and also incorporates ways of dealing with such feelings as anger, sources of help for relationship problems, and conflict resolution skills.

A social studies curriculum provides numerous opportunities for teaching conflict resolution skills through the curriculum. In middle and high schools, students learn about their state, nation and world through the study of history, geography, economics and behavioral sciences. Encountering conflict through the social studies curriculum can lead students to a clearer understanding of past and present causes of conflict.

Through the integration of conflict resolution skills into the guidance curriculum, an appropriate vehicle is available for assisting students in the development of peer mediation skills. The guidance curriculum is also incorporated into components of a conflict resolution model through the grade levels. Skills include: listening, constructive models of expressing feelings, responsible social skills, and distinguishing between anger and aggression.

In a K-12 English-language arts curriculum, students have many opportunities to learn conflict resolution skills. These opportunities come in the form of participation in the safe classroom environment provided by the teacher, participation in cooperative learning and project groups, working on language skills that allows for verbal communication as a vehicle to resolve conflict and express feelings, and directly studying examples of conflict resolution in literature.

Other curricular areas promote skills in such areas as problem solving, interpersonal communication, appreciation and understanding of differences among people and cultures, ethical behavior, and personal responsibility. Subjects such as science, mathematics, vocational education, performing arts, computer science, and information sharing can enhance violence prevention efforts through extension of instruction to illustrate the relationship of the subject matter to the personal behaviors associated with conflict and violence.

For instance, any present mathematics curriculum provides numerous opportunities to practice conflict resolution skills. Problem solving skills are applied, extended, and refined throughout the nine to 12 curriculum. The high school curriculum emphasizes the need for students to apply learned processes to real world situations and problems.

Throughout a science curriculum, several opportunities are available to assist students in developing skills employed in conflict resolution. The science process is necessary to find solutions to problems faced by individuals and society. The high school students explore both the biological and chemical basis of their behavior, especially as behavior relates to conflict resolution.

Vocational education affords students innumerable opportunities to both learn and practice skills which are related to conflict resolution. Vocational programs contribute to students being able to work with others by participating as a team, serving clients or customers, negotiating and functioning amid diversity; to work with and operate effectively within social organizations and technological systems; and develop the capacity to think creatively, make decisions, solve problems, and reason.

The emphasis of the computer skills curriculum on using technology to solve problems provides various opportunities for development of conflict resolution skills and for the use of technology as a medium for accessing information and communicating with others to reach an agreement. As students gain skills in using computer technologies to solve problems, they develop skills common to conflict resolution: identifying facts and issues, generating alternative solutions, and devising solutions to each agreement.

Dance education, like all arts education, deals with both content and processes which support and facilitate safe learning environments. Dance education instructors daily focus on problems with students that call for group decision making, peer mediation, and group problem recognition and problem solving.

Character Education

It is worth repeating what Theodore Roosevelt once said: "To educate a person in mind and not morals is to create a menace to society."

What's wrong with our children today? Why can't they be responsible citizens? It's not nostalgia that provokes this longing; it's a real increase in violence and bad adolescent behavior coupled with the decline in human values and ethics. Teachers put up with shocking levels of aggression and lack of respect.

Character education can be a key to a learning community and for helping our students learn the skills they need to be responsible citizens. One of our biggest responsibilities as educators is to help students develop habits of self-discipline and respect that constitute character. There are numerous books on the market. Hillary Clinton's *It Takes a Village* offers both personal and national examples of the need for character building in our students.

Schools need to assist with teaching children self-discipline. Several states have passed bills which mandate that educational units teach character education development.

Character education is the teaching of traditional civic and moral concepts of altruism, compassion, courage, courtesy, generosity, honesty, industriousness, integrity, loyalty, obedience, punctuality, respect for authority, responsibility, self-discipline, self-respect and tolerance.

Schools may decide to promote a concept a month along the lines of this example:

September—Altruism	February—Honesty
October—Compassion	March—Integrity
November—Courage	April—Loyalty
December—Courtesy	May—Obedience
January—Generosity	June—Respect for authority

Other character education activities:

- Have students prepare public awareness bulletins and service announcements relating to character education.
- Coordinate community service activities.
- Conduct media campaigns stressing the importance of character concepts.
- Ask coaches and athletic directors to promote character in community sport programs.
- Establish a hotline for a safe haven for children. Also, provide a hotline in which parents can call to get information on character

education—volunteers could conduct this at the local schools in the evenings.

• Most importantly, model the concepts of character education.

Character education can be a key not only to a learning community but for gaining public support. Teaching good character and morals is first the responsibility of parents, but it is supported and reinforced by the schools. Character education is moral values in action, and the schools need to address moral behavior. They need to stress to children that they must know the good habits of the mind and of the heart, as well as do good. Good character education is based on universal moral values, and it is the grave mission of the schools to pass on those values to their students.

Law Enforcement Assistance

Although a school may have its own security personnel, establishing a relationship with community law enforcement is essential. Both groups play important roles in making our schools safe. School security personnel are familiar with the school facility, its security devices and the student body. Police officers are trained to deal with violent incidents. Accurate reporting of criminal behaviors to the police sends a clear message that illegal acts will not be tolerated.

In many communities, police officers know the community and its residents. They often have information about community and family problems that is useful to school personnel. They promote school safety by interacting closely with students. Police officers can teach special courses on substance abuse, kidnap prevention, and gun safety, and they often have access to knowledge of community resources such as recreational facilities and organized athletic leagues.

If state and local laws allow, police can assist school administrators in identifying specific students who require additional supervision. In some schools, probation officers work inside the school building where they have better access to the students assigned to them by the courts.

Police officers and juvenile justice authorities need to establish a working relationship with schools. Educators, police and juvenile justice authorities all play an integral part in preventing school crime. Educators are better equipped to teach students. Police are more capable of intervening in a crisis situation involving a violent or potentially violent student. Juvenile justice authorities can assign probation officers and social workers to schools, where they can best monitor and serve adjudicated students, design specific regimens for youthful offenders to influence their behavior, and provide stronger and broader sanctions for violent behavior.

Patrol the school grounds, facilities and travel routes. The presence of police in or near the school and local neighborhoods deters crime and prevents troubling situations from escalating. Police presence disrupts trouble spots that interfere with students traveling to and from school, prevents strangers from entering schools, reduces the ability of students to smuggle weapons to schools, deters gang activity, and identifies students who are selling drugs or are under the influence of drugs. Police can also conduct random searches for weapons or controlled substances, if appropriate. In these and other circumstances, they add their broader authority to the supervision of students.

Respond to reports of criminal activity. When police routinely patrol the school grounds, they are in a better position to act quickly in response to a request for help from school authorities. The role of police in this situation may be to separate a violent student from a potential victim, talk the student into giving up a threatening stance, subdue and transport a student from the scene, contact emergency services, assist in traffic control as emergency services arrive and as parents pick up their children during or after the crisis, collect evidence, or participate in other activities. Rapid response is critical in a situation where many children are in danger.

Consult with school authorities and parents regarding school security. Both juvenile justice authorities and police have specialized training in working with youth. They are aware of effective techniques for modifying the behavior of troubled youth, the appropriate use of rules and sanctions for youths who are chronic offenders, techniques for avoiding violence and victimization, and optional services for troubled students. They are also able to consult more broadly on issues of school, home and personal security. Their information can be shared in school board meetings, community meetings, classrooms, assemblies, printed materials and broadcasts.

Work directly with youth to maintain a constructive relationship. Police and juvenile justice authorities can become involved directly with students outside the police station, classroom, courtroom or other correctional settings. They often develop a good relationship with students as a means of preventing confrontation in the future. As the relationship builds, students see police and juvenile justice authorities as positive role models rather than judges or enforcers, assist them in their work rather than flee from them or hinder their work, and gain a greater understanding about the difficulties they face in their work. Instilling a broader respect for authority is essential in preventing crime. Opportunities for building constructive relationships between authorities and youth include bicycle registration drives, school carnivals, fund-raisers, community policing partnerships, and sponsored recreational activities.

Chapter Four, Parent Involvement in Providing Safe Schools, will give tips on how to recognize violent tendencies in children. Also, preventive techniques and effective practices will be presented.

CHAPTER FOUR

Parent Involvement in Providing Safe Schools

Parents are often left wondering what they did wrong in raising their children and bearing the brunt of the guilt for an entire society. In 1997, 1998 and 1999 alone, we have been confronted with several high profile cases of kids killing kids. West Paducah, Kentucky; Jonesboro, Arkansas; Springfield, Oregon, small town names splashed across the global television screens, unknown but for the notoriety of their children turning on their peers and committing acts only thought to be attributable to adults.

The importance of parental involvement in the lives of children is now needed more than ever before. Parents are the first and most important teachers children have, and they reinforce academic and behavioral lessons taught at school. In addition, parental involvement is extremely important in making schools a safe environment for teaching and learning. School officials must make every effort to promote such parental involvement.

Local school officials should include a "parental involvement plan" in their school system's safe school plans and individual school improvement plans. The parental involvement plan should lay out specific ways to promote and encourage parents to take an active role in the schools.

The North Carolina State Board of Education recommends the following for involving parents in the schools:

- Home visitation should be included in school improvement plans. Teachers—individually or as a team—should visit with parents and students in their homes or some nonschool environment.
- Employers should recognize the importance of parental involvement in schools and adopt or amend their personnel policies to allow parents to volunteer in their children's schools.
- School administrators and teachers need to receive training to help them effectively create and sustain the parent-student-school relationship.
- Appropriate state government agencies need to work together to create a clearinghouse of materials and other resources that local agencies can use to create and implement programs promoting better parenting skills.
- Schools need to examine all available methods for promoting better parent-school communications including web sites and e-mail.

Tips to Get Parents Involved in Schools

Getting parents to participate in anything school related can be a major challenge in today's world. Parents are short on time and energy and often long on outside responsibilities. Betty Anne Coady of Challenger Elementary School in Issaquah, Washington, and Mary Reynolds of Richmond Elementary School in Salem, Oregon, use a variety of methods that are applicable to any school's parent outreach efforts. Here are some of their suggestions:

- Hold meetings on Monday evenings once a month which should be infrequent enough so parents can attend on a regular basis and at a time when parents can be reasonably expected to have gotten home from work.
- Hold dual meetings—once in the day and once in the evenings. That way, parents who work day or night shifts, as well as stay at home parents, could attend.
- Announce programs early and then follow up with a reminder such as a personal letter or a flyer.

- Promote the educational aspect of the program so parents can learn about what their children are being taught in school and how they can help their children.
- Avoid parenting. Instead, teachers need to emphasize that parents are necessary partners in reaching the educational goal of their children.
- Post reminders of upcoming meeting on outside bulletin boards.
- Provide coffee and snacks at the first meeting and let parents organize refreshments for subsequent meetings.
- Provide childcare services. Teacher assistants or volunteers can serve in this area.
- Don't use these meetings to corner parents to discuss concerns about individual children. The parents should be the focus. There is a time and a place for discussing their children, but it's not when they are attending volunteer functions.

Parent Involvement Reduces School's Behavioral Problems

Discipline is a large part of any school administrator's job. This was especially true for Martha Roten when she became principal at Noralto Elementary in Sacramento, California. The school is located in the poorest part of town where half the battle is getting kids to school and past the temptations of drugs and gangs.

Not only does Roten get the kids to school but now parents are coming to school. To involve parents in the school was something she decided to focus on eight years ago after conferring with the school counselor and outreach coordinator. She believes her students deserve the credit for getting their parents immersed in the educational process. Many parents have honed their own parenting skills through their involvement at the school.

The biggest change to come from parent involvement is the reduction of behavioral problems. The school now has the fewest suspensions; prior to the parent involvement, it had the highest. Discipline problems have dropped from 50 percent to between 5 percent and 10 percent. As the family connected to the school, the behavioral problems of the child were eliminated.

Parent involvement at the school ranges from attending programs to volunteering for office or schoolyard duty. Some parents work in the after-school program.

Studies of individual families show that what the family does is more important to student success than family income or education and is the best long-term investment a family can make. When parents become involved in their children's education in a positive way, children achieve higher grades and test scores, have better attendance, complete more homework, demonstrate more positive attitudes and behavior, graduate at higher rates, and have greater enrollment in higher education.

Parents can become involved in their children's academic/school success by:

- Spending quality time with them and taking an interest in their success.
- Accepting responsibility for their academic success.
- Establishing rules and limitations at home and being consistent in rewarding and punishing.
- Understanding and stressing in the home the importance of following school rules and procedures.
- Being knowledgeable of state laws (N.C. House Bill 1008— proper storage of firearms, other school safety and crime prevention laws, school attendance laws, and so on) pertaining to their responsibilities as parents.
- Setting high expectations for their children.
- Teaching them good work habits, values, and to respect themselves and others.
- Respecting their children and sharing with them the importance of education.
- Supervising and monitoring homework and staying informed about their children's progress.
- Serving on activity committees, policy-making boards and volunteering time or resources for school functions.

Parenting Practices

Children often receive mixed messages from parents and other adults about what is right and what is wrong. The use of material goods to persuade children to behave in one way or to dissuade them from behaving in another is one example of sending a mixed message. In such situations, children are bribed by promises of expensive clothing or toys. In addition, today's youth seem surprised when asked if they are required to perform chores in and around their home. Teachers commonly report that students relate to them that their parents have told them that they do not have to do what the teacher says, and that if anyone tries to take something from them or insults them or hits them, they should fight. Unfortunately, many parents admit that they have so instructed their children and are offended that teachers question such directions.

These types of parenting are evident across the socioeconomic spectrum. Parenting that indulges, neglects, abuses, or ignores children, and that fails to provide strong, positive guidance, discipline, and nurturing, contributes to the spread of violence in schools. Such parenting is seen in families plagued by chronic unemployment and poverty, especially when parents are concentrating more on the economic survival of the family than on the attitudes and behavior of the children. It is also seen in affluent families that indulge their children's every material request. Lately, it is seen in families where parents do not have quality time to spend with their children because of their job demands.

Thirty-six percent of students report that lack of parental supervision at home is the major factor contributing to violence in schools. However, 34 percent of them cited as a second major factor gang or group membership or peer pressure. Several recent studies concluded that peer group pressure is perhaps the fastest and most disturbing cause of acts of violence among youth, whether in or out of school.

Examining Families

Frequently, children's destructive, abusive, or deadly behavior is not restricted to the school. Many of these disturbed juveniles show chronic patterns of violence at home or in the wider family unit. Commonly asked questions about such children include:

1. What are the parents like?
2. Are the parents responsible?
3. Do the parents seem to care?
4. Are the parents loving and do they reciprocate love?
5. Are they aware of what their children are doing?

6. Are the parents credible?
7. Is there a lot of tension, stress, or trauma in the family?
8. Is there a family history of domestic violence?
9. Is there a history of abuse?
10. How does the family resolve disputes?
11. Do they resort to violence?
12. Is there communication among family members?
13. Do the parents expect the school system or justice system or society to raise their children?
14. Are the parents afraid of the child?
15. How does the child get along with family members?

Parents must be held accountable at all times; negligent, abusive, or inappropriate parenting can no longer be ignored. The parents must also have effective resources to assist them at times with disturbed children. Here is where community mobilization can benefit everyone (this will be discussed in detail in Chapter Five). The sooner we identify these troubled children, the sooner we can help them before they develop into deadly individuals.

What Parents Can Do

While it may be unfair to blame parents for their children's violent behavior, particularly when those parents are victims of violence too, it's important to note what parents can do to raise healthy, responsible, and nonviolent children. Parents need to be more proactive in their approach to raising children, says John Covey, director of the Home and Family Division of Franklin Covey Company and a former member of the Utah State Board of Education. According to Covey, family is not enough of a priority for too many people; the shaping of children's lives often is too subject to the forces of our wider culture, and the values of that culture—expressed in the popular media—are having too great an influence on children. Parents really are no longer raising their children; the media have control of what is happening in the home. Parents need to take a more active role in shaping the values for their children. Parents can do this by turning off the media and spending more one on one time with them. Essentially, if parents will be more active in their children's lives, and pay more attention to them, then children will be happier, healthier, have better values, and will be less violent.

Parents have to be confident that if they communicate to their children a strong sense of their own values and morals, then their children will develop those same values and morals. Parents can do this by developing a relationship of trust. Parents have to demonstrate to their children how to make and keep commitments, and to apologize when appropriate. They have to give their children a sense of direction, mentoring them by spending time one on one with them. As family life becomes more defined in these ways, children begin to trust the structure. When one develops a child in this way, they learn to give and to serve and that work is a spiritual necessity. They come to feel secure and to trust. They live by principles and know what those principles are. In essence, by spending time with children, by developing a relationship of trust, parents convey a sense of value and importance to their children. This alone can make a world of difference in the life of a child, and can reduce the chances of a child becoming violent.

What Do You Do If Your Child Has Violent Tendencies?

Even in situations where parents have done the best they can in raising a child, that child may begin to show signs of acting violently and posing a threat to others. In those cases, parents, community and educators face significant challenges. Often their best recourse is making sure these children gain access to the many social and psychological services that exist today to help troubled youth.

Other tips:

- Discuss the school's discipline policy with your child. Show you support the rules and procedures.
- Involve your child in setting rules for appropriate behavior at home.
- Help you child find ways to show anger that does not involve verbally or physically hurting others. Serve as a role model especially when you get angry or upset.
- Help your child understand the value of accepting individual differences and cultural values.
- Note any disturbing behaviors in your child. You might want to review the profiles of children with violent tendencies in Chapter Two.

- Frequent behavioral problems at school can be signs of a serious problem. Get help for your child. Talk with professionals, such as the school psychologist or counselor. Show support for your child but do not excuse their inappropriate behavior and most importantly, do not make excuses for such behavior.
- Keep lines of communication open with your child. Encourage your child to let you know where and with whom they will be. Get to know your child's friends.
- Listen to your child when they tell you things about their friends or children they know who may be exhibiting troubling behavior. Share this information with appropriate people.
- Be involved in your child's school life by supporting and reviewing homework, talking with their teachers, and attending school functions such as parent conferences, class programs, open houses and PTA meetings.
- Volunteer to work with school-based groups concerned with violence prevention and intervention.
- Find out if a violence prevention and intervention group exists in your community. Offer to participate in the group's activities.

Internet Guidelines

The Internet is like fire—a wonder and a danger, with ability to enhance lives dramatically or destroy them. Reams of valuable information are available at the touch of our fingers on a keyboard. So are pornographers, instructions on how to make a bomb, and sexual predators who can lure children through chat rooms or e-mail.

We are living in the age when many children know more about computers than their parents; the caring adults in their lives need to learn about technology and its potential for danger and violence.

Whether families own computers or not, their children will be exposed to the Internet through access at a friend's home, in the schools, or at the local library. Schools and public libraries do have some protections on their systems to prevent access to certain materials.

While some adults are apathetic toward new technology or are intimidated by it, predators and pornographers are getting smarter, developing ways to lure children onto their sites.

Parents and guardians who have computers and Internet access at home particularly cannot afford to let technology get ahead of them.

Whether they know a lot or a little about technology, however, there are several things they can do to protect their families:

- Place the computer in a family room, such as the dining room, den or living room, where the family congregates together. This will discourage children from browsing sites where danger lurks. It will help parents remain aware of what their children are viewing.
- Ask children to teach the family about the Internet. Since the younger generation is more knowledgeable, respect that knowledge and use it to the family's advantage.
- Remain aware of young people's activities in "chat rooms," where they can converse electronically with people from all over the world. Know who they are talking to, and about what, to help protect them from predators.
- Research blocking programs that can be purchased and used to limit the sites in which children have access. While this is not a perfect solution or a replacement for parents' personal interest in their children's computer activities, it can be a tool to help manage the Internet.

These simple guidelines are not enough, however, in an age when technology is racing ahead. If forums to help adults protect the children in our country are held near you, attend them. Also, for immediate advice, call the schools and find out what's available in the way of workshops or in-services for parents.

Television Viewing

The average elementary age child spends 30 hours per week viewing television. By 16, the average child will have witnessed 200,000 acts of violence and by 18, approximately 40,000 sexually explicit scenes.

Ninety-eight percent of American homes have at least one television set, which is watched each week for an average of 28 hours by children between the ages of two and 11, and 23 hours by teenagers. Children who grow up in lower-income families, with fewer organized activities, watch more television than their more affluent peers do. Children admit that certain television shows encourage them to engage in sexual activity before they are ready, behave aggressively, and to be disrespectful to adults. Eighty percent of Americans who responded to a 1993 Times-Mirror Poll said they believed television was harmful to society and especially to children. Why do parents or guardians continue to allow their children to watch so much television? Children become immune to violence because they have watched so much on television. What most children are seeing on television can't be good for them (Clinton, 1996).

George Gerbner, former dean of the Annenberg School of Communication at the University of Pennsylvania and founder of the Media-Research Cultural Indicators Project and the International Cultural Environment Movement, is profiled in an article in the May 1997 *Atlantic* written by Scott Stossel. Gerber says that violence is about power; that violence on television serves as a lesson of power that puts people in their places.

Gerbner further explains that we live in a world which is erected by the stories we tell and, by extension, it is erected by the stories we are told. This is changing; the stories we are told now are not told to us by our parents, school, church or community but by a relatively small group of global conglomerates with something to sell. This alters in a very fundamental way the cultural environment into which our children are born, grow up, and become socialized.

Defenders of television argue that children are subjected to violence in other media—including fairy tales and other literary classics. However, the tradition of storytelling embodied in fairy tales and modern children's literature assists in developing in children a moral base.

Parents can help keep their children from being exposed to violence on television by establishing some parameters. These might include:

- No television before school.
- No television after dinner.
- No television during dinner.
- Nobody can sit too close to the television.
- No fighting over the best seat for television viewing or channels to watch.
- Television is only for weekends.
- No turning the channel when someone else is watching.
- The television can only be on until 9:30 each night.
- You can't turn on the television just because you're bored.
- Only two shows a day.
- No television that's really scary.

Effects of Media Violence on Children

Media violence:

- Causes an increase in mean-spirited, aggressive behavior.
- Causes increased levels of fearfulness, mistrust, and self-protective behavior toward others.
- Contributes to desensitization and callousness to the effects of violence and the suffering of others.
- Provides violent heroes whom children seek to emulate.
- Provides children justification for resorting to violence when they think they are right.
- Creates an increasing appetite for viewing more violence and more extreme violence.
- Fosters a culture in which disrespectful behavior becomes a legitimate way for people to treat each other.

Guidelines for Helping Children Deal with Violence in the News

- Trusted adults play a vital role in helping children sort out what they have heard and need to figure out. Let children know it's okay to raise these kinds of issues with you. Older children might benefit from a regular time built into the week when they can raise and talk about these issues.
- Don't expect young children to understand violence as adults do. When you work on these issues with children, try to find out as much as you can about what each individual child knows and understands or is struggling to understand. Then base your responses on what you find out.
- When children hear about something scary or disturbing, they sometimes relate it to themselves and start to worry about their own safety. Even when you cannot make a situation better, reassure children about their safety—for instance say, "That can't happen to you because your parents have always ____." This kind of reassurance is what children most need to hear.
- Answer questions and clear up misconceptions but do not try to give children all the information available about a news story. The best guide is to follow the child's lead, giving small pieces

of information at a time and seeing how the child responds, before deciding what to say next.

- Look for opportunities to help children learn alternatives to the violence they hear about on the news. One effective way to do this is to point to examples from the children's own experiences. For instance, you might say, "I really get angry when people solve their own problems by hurting each other. Remember when you got really angry with Gary for ___? You didn't hurt him. You told him ___." It is also important to make positive conflict resolution a regular part of the week.

- Recognize and support young children's efforts to work out what they have heard through their play, drawing and other activities. This, regardless of anything else you can do, can play a very therapeutic role for children.

- Keep teachers and school counselors informed about your efforts to work with your children on troubling news events.

Violent Media and Stimulus Addiction

Dr. Paul Gathercoal, media literary expert at Gustavus Adolphus College in St. Peter, Minnesota, explains how fast-paced, violent television and video games may be habit-forming and eventually addictive. He draws upon recent brain research on the chemical-neurological connection and makes these important points:

- The difference between drug addiction and stimulus addiction is that with stimulus addiction the drugs (endorphins) are already inside the body; they simply need to be released.

- These endorphins are released in response to stress and to emotional experiences.

- An optimum level of endorphin release is maintained through everyday social interaction with the environment and its people, its challenges, its beauty and the successes and stresses of life.

- When a stimulus is emotion laden, new and exciting, the brain's reticular activating system alerts the cerebral cortex that this is worth special notice, and undivided attention is given to the stimulus. Many media messages, especially violent images, have by their very nature the characteristics of being emotionally provocative and exciting.

- Constant and prolonged exposure to fast-paced violent media can affect children in two ways. First, they may become addicted to these endorphin-activating stimuli. They may actually physically need their daily fix of media violence. Second, they can build up immunity to media induced emotional stresses and become incapable of producing socially acceptable emotional responses in the real world.

What Do You Do If Your Child Is Addicted to Violent Media?

It is imperative to keep young children away from violent media, especially, violent video games. Start children out with television programs and videos and analytic, nonviolent, computer and video games. Make sure they use their heads more than their trigger fingers.

Violent and Analytic Video Games

Learning higher order thinking skills, like problem solving, planning and organizing, is an important developmental task during early adolescence. Analytic video games such as puzzles, mazes, treasure hunts, and stimulation games can help develop these types of skills. Violent video games, however, which rely almost entirely on the player's reflex responses, may develop hand-eye coordination, but will provide very little practice for higher-level thinking skills. Over time, some children may become habituated to this nonthinking, quick response model of problem solving. Without adequate mental practice during this developmental time in a child's life, the child's ability to acquire mature higher thinking skills and effective problem-solving abilities may be compromised.

Video Games Send the Following Messages...

- Problems can be resolved quickly with little personal investment.
- The best way to solve a problem is to eliminate the source of the problem.

- Look at problems in terms of black and white, right or wrong.
- Use instinctual behaviors to react to problems, not thoughtful behavior.
- Personal imagination is not an important problem-solving skill.
- It is acceptable to not question the game's rule-driven reality.

Contrast the above with what children can learn from analytic video games:

- Problems are solved through patience, personal initiative, perseverance, and tolerance.
- Gathering information requires work and thinking through ideas.
- Defining and solving problems involves complex thinking skills.
- A solution in one instance may not work as a solution in another instance.
- Skills such as planning actions, organizing information, predicting outcomes, experimenting with trial solutions, evaluating solutions and their consequences are important skills.
- Use personally generated thoughtful responses to solve problems.
- Use imagination and thinking abilities to cocreate, with the game's writer, inventive situations.

Most parents can see the importance of monitoring video games and violence media. Be sure you know what video games your child is playing with and constantly evaluate them for appropriateness. The market is flooded with violent video games and they are very enticing to adolescents. It's your responsibility as a parent to make sure your child is not overexposed to violence.

Weapons

Guns and other weapons clearly are a hazard to a safe learning environment and the welfare of human beings. According to the National Center for Health Statistics, every day 14 young people, age 19 and under, are killed as a result of gun use. According to the "Metropolitan Life Survey of the American Teacher, 1993; Violence in America's Public Schools," 11 percent of teachers and 23 percent of students say they have been victims of violence in or near their schools. While the elimination of guns and weapons from school is the responsibility of all segments of the school and society, parents specifically can assist in eliminating weapons from the school grounds by:

- Teaching their children about the dangers and consequences of guns and weapons, and keeping all guns and weapons in the household under lock and key and away from children.
- Supporting the school's policies to eliminate guns and weapons and working with the school to develop programs to prevent violence.
- Checking bookbags and other belongings for weapons or guns.
- Teaching children how to solve disagreements without resorting to violence.
- Following school guidelines in reporting guns and weapons seen or heard of to the appropriate adult.

America Under the Gun

As we begin the 21st century, reports of violence in our schools and offices seem to be coming at us at an alarming rate. A *Newsweek* poll found that 81 percent of respondents believe gun-related violence in schools has increased in recent years. The blame is placed on a variety of factors: poor parenting (57 percent), violence in the media (52 percent), the prejudice and preaching of hate groups (46 percent), and the increased availability of guns and other weapons (48 percent).

There are more than 200 million guns in circulation in the United States, and more than a third of American households have one. About two thirds (64 percent) of respondents with kids under 18 were very or somewhat concerned about their kids being harmed or getting into trouble while visiting their friends' homes. Sixty-two percent thought it was very or somewhat likely that a shooting incident could happen in their community. Despite their concerns, many have doubts about the effectiveness of tougher gun-control laws.

Theories differ about where young people get their guns. School security experts and law enforcement officials estimate that 80 percent of the firearms students bring to school come from the home, while students estimate that 40 percent of their peers who bring guns to school buy them on the street (54 percent). The Chicago-based Joyce Foundation commissioned Louis Harris Research, Inc., to conduct a poll which found that only 43 percent of parents who own a gun and have children under 18 years of age keep those guns safely locked (55 percent). An estimated 1.2 million elementary-aged children, latchkey kids, have access to guns in their homes (56 percent). Therefore, one way to reduce youth violence may be to restrict the flow of handguns to adults.

There have been several proposals about parents being liable and accountable if their children commit a violent crime. At this time, there are mixed feelings about what this would accomplish. Anyone whose child commits a heinous crime, like the parents in Littleton, suffers their own brand of punishment—greater than anything legally punishable does.

A good resource on gun-violence is an educational packet offered by the National Emergency Medicine Association. The program is over a year old and recently there has been a lot of interest in it. The intent of the program is to stress the consequences of gun violence among youth. It portrays scenarios in which children might encounter a gun, and then it shows what happens when guns are used: the disfigurement, the pain of therapy and rehabilitation, and the emotional pain that gun violence causes friends and family. Parents might check with their schools to see if they have or can obtain the program. The program is very useful and appropriate at PTA and community meetings.

Drugs

We cannot educate our children in schools where drugs threaten their safety. For students to learn well, their schools must be disciplined and feel safe. While most schools do provide a secure learning environment, a growing number of communities—urban, suburban, and rural—are experiencing problems with violence and with alcohol and drug use.

What Can Parents Do?

Parents play a huge role in the interconnected social tapestry of raising children successfully. Research shows that kids view parents as their most influential role models. A study also shows that 74 percent of all fourth graders wish their parents would talk to them about drugs.

Overwhelmingly, research demonstrates that kids want parents to be parents, and that is the best deterrent in the fight against drugs.

Spending time with your children—talking about their friends, school, and activities; asking them what they think about anything from music to Columbine—is a proven deterrent to drug use. Research shows that knowing your children, who they hang out with and their parents as well, dramatically reduces the likelihood that they will get in trouble with drugs. Another effective deterrent is praising and rewarding them for good behavior. Tell your children you love them. Go out for pizza or have the family sit down at the table for a meal instead of watching television. Get to know the music your child listens to and let them talk about the lyrics: are they really appropriate language; do they contain violent themes? Keeping children drug-free is achieved in a series of small, personal ways.

Family Violence

Current research now shows that children who witness family violence act in a similar way to those children who have personally experienced abuse. Outwardly, they tend to be more aggressive and antisocial, with problems of anger and temper. Inwardly, children tend to be fearful, inhibited, anxious, depressed and in general have a low self-esteem. Generally, boys tend to act out more than girls; girls tend to internalize more than boys. Preschool children often regress and act younger. Infants often suffer from attachment disorder and are not able to bond with their parents.

So what can be done in the way of prevention and intervention? Children can be taught to contact 911 and the appropriate information to give. They can have a plan for a safe place to go (their bedroom or a neighbor's home). Teaching children not to intervene during a violent situation is imperative. Some violence is a learned behavior; therefore, children can be taught conflict resolution skills and encouraged to find peaceful ways to solve conflicts. Teaching little ones verbal skills such as "No, that is mine" or "Stop that, you're hurting me" is better that hitting or pushing or bullying in the situation.

For those children who have already been exposed to family violence, they need to be able to talk about those scary events or act them out. Those children are in need of a trusting and nurturing adult relationship to heal the insecurities resulting from family violence. A structured and predictable home environment will help the child who has been in a chaotic or dangerous environment. Predictable daily routine will allay the fear and mistrust that the child has already developed.

Violence is not a simple cause-and-effect event. It is a multidimensional event affecting all who directly or indirectly experience it. Children trust adults to protect them, and they deserve to live and learn in a safe environment.

Warning Signs of Children Living in a Violent Home

- Unusual or unexplained injuries, or injuries which are at different stages of healing.
- Chronic illnesses, headaches or stomachaches.
- Signs of neglect, such as poor hygiene or dirty clothing.
- Withdrawal (for example, playing alone and having no friends).
- Depression or low self-esteem.
- Use of violence to solve conflict.
- Sleeping too little, too much or during school.
- Flashbacks or nightmares.
- Difficulty expressing emotions other than anger.
- School problems, including lengthy absences.
- Acting overly responsible (as if the child is the adult in the family).

Warning Signs for Teenagers

- Running away from home or dropping out of school.
- Sexually transmitted diseases, teen pregnancy or prostitution.
- Joining a gang, committing crimes, using weapons.
- Problems with alcohol, tobacco or other drugs.
- Talking about or attempting suicide.

Warning Signs for Preschool Children

- Frequent crying.
- Wanting to be held all the time or stiffening when held.

- Frequent hitting, biting or kicking.
- Stuttering.
- Regression (return to thumb sucking or bed-wetting).

Warning Signs for School-Age Children

- Trouble concentrating at school.
- Unusual knowledge of sex or violence for their age.
- Fighting, bullying or self-abuse.
- Stealing, cheating or lying.
- Regression (seeking constant attention, using baby talk).

What Can Parents Do?

- Be role models. Many children who grew up with violence credit a relative or friend's parent with showing them a better way and giving them love.
- Family support. Being close to brothers, sisters or other relatives helps children feel loved and needed.
- Community support. Positive youth activities and mentoring programs give children a chance to learn new skills. It also helps them have a sense of purpose in life and build self-esteem.
- Therapy. Can help family members rebuild self-esteem, learn to trust again and develop healthy ways to express emotions. Therapy for children may include play therapy, drawing and one on one counseling.

National PTA Addresses School Violence

In response to incidents of school-based violence across the country, National PTA President Lois Jean White issued a call to action to the 6.5 million members. She has charged PTAs to take the lead in bringing communities together to discuss school violence and the deeper issues driving children to commit violent acts. The National PTA developed a new Community Violence Prevention kit to help PTAs organize town meetings and community forums on this issue. Each new PTA president will receive this booklet as part of the annual resources for PTAs. The information can also be found on the National PTA's website at www.pta.org/events/violprev.

Our children are anesthetized to violence, to pain, to guilt. Television programs, video games and movies numb children to reality. Statements that movies contribute to the problem anger moviemakers. Partly, they are justified; we cannot blame the crisis entirely on the television and movie industry. We cannot blame it entirely on the media. We cannot blame it entirely on the availability of guns, either.

Listening to debates rage on all sides, the crisis with our youth is the fault of so many diverse elements. Each industry fights to protect itself, feeling the problem is not of its doing. What they and we fail to see is the whole thing—listening to only parts of a conversation can be misleading ... looking at only parts of an issue can be deadly.

As parents, educators, peers, and legislatures come to terms with the violent tragedies taking place among our youth, someone must step back from the pain, the shock, and the confusion and see the whole situation. All too often, though, we race frantically for someone to blame. We've lived in complacency for so long that we want, we need, to have someone else solve our problems for us.

How many children must die in their schools, on their streets, in their homes before we wake up and take charge?

Stop allowing your children to watch violence and death in their entertainment. Give up some of what you may want in order to give your children socially, positive programming choices.

Monitor the music and the video games and the Internet sites your children use. Don't give in and allow your children to do what they want because it's easy. Some music is just too harmful, some video games too deadly, some web sites too angry.

Love your children and show them this love in the way you are raising them. Be good role models—tiny eyes and ears are always watching and listening.

Chapter Five, "Schools, Parents, and Communities Working Together," provides strategies for creating a school community, community involvement, community needs assessment, and collaboration. Also in the chapter, an example of collaboration within a community is shared.

CHAPTER FIVE

Schools, Parents, and Communities Working Together

The vast majority of the nation's schools are safe places. However, some schools do have serious crime and violence problems that compromise the learning environment and endanger children and teachers. Schools cannot effectively deal with these problems without significant communitywide support. Many communities are successfully reducing school crime and violence by adopting comprehensive, integrated communitywide plans that promote healthy childhood development and address the problems of school violence and alcohol and other drug abuse. However, these communities are the exception, not the rule. In the spring of 1999, President Clinton announced the Safe Schools/Healthy Students Initiative, a unique grant program jointly administered by the U.S. Departments of Education, Health and Human Resources, and Justice. The initiative promotes comprehensive, integrated communitywide strategies for school safety and healthy child development across the country. These strategies provide students, schools and communities the benefit of enhanced educational, mental health, social, law enforcement, and, as appropriate, juvenile justice system services that can bolster healthy childhood development and prevent violence and alcohol and other drug abuse.

121

The Safe Schools/Healthy Students Initiative draws on the best practices of the education, justice, social services, and mental health systems to promote a comprehensive, integrated problem-solving process for use by communities in addressing school violence. This process, which was highlighted in the Initiative's 1998 Annual Report, includes 1. establishing school-community partnerships; 2. identifying and measuring the problem; 3. setting measurable goals and objectives; 4. identifying appropriate research-based programs and strategies; 5. implementing programs and strategies in an integrated fashion; 6. evaluating the outcomes of programs and strategies; and 7. revising the plan on the basis of evaluated information.

The initiative requires comprehensive, integrated and communitywide plans to address at least the following six elements: 1. safe school environment; 2. prevention and early intervention programs that address violence, alcohol and other drugs; 3. school and community mental health prevention and treatment intervention services; 4. early childhood psychological and emotional development programs; 5. educational reform; and 6. safe school policies. Plans must be developed in partnership with, at a minimum, the local educational agency, local public mental health authority, local law enforcement agency, family members, students and juvenile justice officials.

Fifty-four Safe Schools/Healthy Students Initiative grants have been awarded to local educational agencies in partnership with local law enforcement and public mental health authorities. Awards range from up to $3 million per year for urban school districts, to up to $2 million per year for suburban school districts and up to $1 million per year for rural school districts and tribal schools.

The initiative grant is a good example of collaboration which is taking place throughout the United States to combat the violence in our schools and communities.

Presidential Call to Action

President Clinton announced a series of new initiatives that address many of the problems identified in the Annual Report on School Safety, including:

- A New Federal Response to Violent Deaths in Schools. The President proposed a $12 million School Emergency Response to

Violence—Project SERV—to help schools and local communities respond to school-related violent deaths.

- Targeted Resources for Schools with Serious Crime Problems. The President announced a new initiative to hire up to 2,000 community police and school resource officers to work in the 10 percent of schools with serious crime problems and train police, educators, and other members of the community to help recognize the early warning signs of violence.
- Reforms to Help Make All Schools Safe, Disciplined, and Drug-Free. The President announced his intent to overhaul the Safe and Drug-Free Schools and Communities Program so that schools will be required to adopt rigorous, comprehensive school safety plans for effective drug and violence prevention and reduction.
- A Communitywide Response to School Safety and Youth Violence. The President announced the launch of a new Safe Schools/Safe Communities Initiative designed to help 10 cities develop and implement communitywide school safety plans.
- A New Partnership to Engage Youth in Solutions to Violence. Together with Music Television (MTV), the federal government launched a new campaign to encourage young people to become mentors and help their peers resolve conflicts peacefully. This campaign, "Fight for Your Rights; Take a Stand Against Youth Violence," reached millions of young people and helped make our schools and communities safer.

Each of these programs has a common element—collaboration with the community.

Creating a School Community

Marshfield Senior High School, in the Oregon coast port of Coos Bay, might seem vulnerable to the spread of gangs. Due to the transient nature of many jobs in the local economy, the high school consistently experiences a 30 percent annual turnover in student population. The famous Raiders jackets are visible, and new students occasionally boast about being gang members. However, no gang activity has developed because, according to Principal Arnold Roblan, Marshfield High has made a concerted effort to fill the needs that cause young people to turn to gangs.

The school has worked very hard to create a sense of community for its students. Two years ago a new method was adopted to help achieve this goal: the Natural Helpers Program. Originally developed in the state of Washington, the program is based on identifying existing natural support programs.

Students are asked to list the people in the school they would talk to if they had a problem, both fellow students and adults. The names of the individuals repeatedly mentioned are collected, and a group representing a cross-section of them is invited to a weekend retreat. These Natural Helpers are given training in active listening and problem-solving skills, including how to recognize when the problem is beyond their ability to solve. The group meets on a biweekly basis for the rest of the school year to work on additional intervention and communication skills.

Providing Job Opportunities

Job opportunities are crucial for older adolescents. There is evidence to support the fact that gang youth would choose reputable employment over crime if they had the option. Unfortunately, they usually don't have the skills and attitudes to hold good jobs. Schools may steer youths away from crime by providing job training or referrals to jobs in the community.

For example, Portland Public Schools works with the Private Industry Council to provide job-related programs for high-risk youths. Students are given special counseling and are ready for job interviews.

After-Hours Programs in Schools

A good cost-efficient and effective crime prevention strategy is to have children participate in after-school programs and athletic events. Again and again studies have found that after-school recreational programs which aggressively recruit youth and sustain their participation in their programs hold excellent potential to prevent juvenile delinquency within the community.

Another example of effective after-school programs which provide an opportunity for youth to resist being drawn into delinquent behavior are the "Beacon," or full-service, schools operating successfully in New York. As children are increasingly raised in families with both parents working or by single working parents, crime data reveal that the hours between the end of school supervision and the beginning of parental supervision (3:00 P.M. until 8:00 P.M.) are peak juvenile crime hours. For many of these children, the result of closing schools immediately after the school day ends is leaving children alone on the streets.

Full-service schools address the dilemma by productively occupying children during those peak crime hours in educational, recreational or counseling activities. These are currently existing schools which in some communities are the most resource-rich settings. By staying open late, they are able to provide a relatively low-cost response to juvenile crime that does not restrict children's freedom, provides them with recreational and educational opportunities, and enhances our communities in the process.

Riley Announces $34.6 Million in Grants to Train Drug and Safety Coordinators in Middle Schools

That ninety-seven school districts in three states would be able to recruit, hire and train middle school drug prevention and school safety coordinators under nearly $35 million in grants was announced on September 30, 1999, by then U.S. Secretary of Education, Richard W. Riley.

The three-year grants were awarded to school districts and consortia of smaller districts with significant drug, discipline and violence problems in middle schools.

"Research shows that in order to make an impact on students, prevention programs must include in-school prevention coordinators—preferably on-the-job full-time," said Riley. "This $35 million will support intervention efforts in middle schools that can make a long-term impact on reducing youth drug use and creating safer schools.

Middle schools and students will benefit by using coordinators to:

- Identify and assist schools in adopting successful, research-based drug and violence prevention programs and strategies.
- Develop, coordinate and analyze assessments of school drug and crime problems.
- Work with community organizations, parents and students to ensure collaboration.

- Identify additional funding sources for drug prevention and school safety program initiatives.
- Provide feedback to state educational agencies on successful programs and activities.

Community Involvement

Now, more than ever, there is a need for schools and the community to work in a concerted team effort in planning for safer schools. The community includes a network of agencies that provide services essential for a safe school.

Schools should seek the assistance and expertise of other organizations in planning activities and implementing strategies to reduce violence. Often, the lack of interagency collaboration causes the comprehensive needs of students to go unmet. Schools can take the lead in seeking to establish collaborative relationships with other agencies so violence can be reduced and eliminated.

Organizing Community Efforts

Parents, school officials and community members working together can be the most effective way to prevent violence. According to the National Crime Prevention Council, the crime rate can decrease by as much as 30 percent when a violence prevention initiative is a communitywide effort.

Steps to Organizing a Community Forum:

- Create an action team or committee.
- Identify priority issues and focus.
- Develop a plan and set goals.
- Identify stakeholders.
- Determine format and logistics of event.
- Secure commitments of support.
- Invite speakers.
- Plan publicity and media coverage.
- Hold the event.
- Evaluate effort and follow up.

Create an Action Team or Committee

Call a meting of your PTA or parent advisory board or form a special committee to discuss organizing a town meeting or community forum. Your committee may include PTA officers or members, parent advisory council members, Booster Club members, educators and officials, business and community leaders, and others who have a stake in safeguarding children against violence in your community.

Identify Priority Issues and Focus

The committee should identify the priority issues and needs of families and schools in your community to help you choose the focus of the forum. Could the main purpose or focus of the forum be to: identify problems and possible solutions; evaluate current programs and services and make changes or improvements; identify needed programs and who could implement them; find funding sources or continued support for violence prevention initiatives? Any one of these things—or a combination of a few—would work as a focus for your forum.

Develop a Plan and Set Goals

Set goals for the forum—those things you hope will result from this meeting. Make goals realistic and achievable. The forum body should be asked to make a commitment to pursue these goals. Identify what each organization can do and by when. Then plan for a follow-up meeting. This part of the step will become clear as stakeholders and organizations are identified.

Identify Stakeholders

Identify the stakeholders within your community who would have an interest in participating in a forum. Identify the groups of citizens within the community who have the ability to influence public action, opinion, policy decisions, or who have a stake in the outcome. Within each group of citizens are organizations that serve the interests of the members of the groups they support. Determine what organizations or community leaders should be represented in your forum. Consider having the following members of your school and community involved in your forum:

- Other parent- or child-related groups or organizations.
- Principals, deans of students, teachers, school counselors, psychologists, nurses and social workers.

- Local board of education members, and other education-focused groups.
- Public health and mental health professionals.
- Pediatricians and family practitioners, health organizations, crisis intervention outreach workers.
- Local business owners.
- Chamber of commerce members.
- Adult trainers in conflict resolution or youths trained in peer mediation.
- Police officers, probation officers and other law enforcement personnel.
- Juvenile and family court judges or other juvenile justice personnel.
- Leaders of neighborhood crime watch units, or other crime prevention groups.
- City council officers, the mayor, other elected officials.
- Members of community organizations such as United Way, YMCA, Big Brothers and Big Sisters.
- Staff of the regional centers for Drug-Free Schools and Communities of the U.S. Department of Education.
- Senior citizen groups, day-care facility personnel, park district leaders.
- Area council of churches, officials from synagogues, mosques and other places of worship, ministerial alliance.

The criteria for participation may include:

1. The group or organization has a genuine concern about the issue.
2. The member or organization is respected and known in the community.
3. The group is compatible in philosophy and beliefs.
4. The group's approach to addressing the issue fits with that of the rest of the members.

Select a contact person for each group or organization; decide who will contact them and what will be said. Determine each group's interest and level of participation. Ask for suggestions for speakers.

Determine Format and Logistics of Event

Determine the format of your forum. How many members will attend? Who will be invited to speak? Will each organization or group represented speak or have input? How long will the forum last? Will members rotate? Define responsibilities of group members.

Once the format and interest level have been determined, establish a date, time and place for meetings. Make arrangements for the meeting place and for other aspects such as refreshments, parking, special visual slides, and other items.

Secure Commitments of Support

For success, have all forum participants identify what resources their group will provide to lend support. Identify all needed materials and financial sources that will be available to the group (rental fees, postage, and so on). Also, select a chairperson to manage the event. A recorder needs to be designated and minutes need to be kept for each meeting.

Invite Speakers

From among the organizations that have shown interest and agreed to lend support, determine who will address the major issues of concern. Once you've identified your potential speakers, invite them to present at a forum. Include in the invitation an explanation of the focus of the forum, what the speaker should address, length of speech, and other details such as time, place and date.

Plan Publicity and Media Coverage

Develop a good public relations plan. Use community newspapers, radio and television stations to keep the public informed of what is taking place at the forum and for announcing meeting dates and times.

Hold the Event

Finalize plans for the forum. Have an established agenda and follow it. Ask someone to record the minutes from the forum or videotape the event and make the video available for others to review.

Evaluate Efforts and Follow Up

Be sure to send thank you notes to speakers and send follow-up information to the organizations that attended. Begin work on setting up an evaluation meeting. Notify the media of what the group did and what the next steps will be.

Community Needs Assessment

One of the first tasks the planning committee can do is conduct a community needs assessment. The assessment will be helpful in identifying local problems, the causes and the solutions. Topics for the checklist might include:

- Parenting courses on communication skills, discipline and children's self-esteem.
- Parent workshops on helping children deal with media violence.
- Conflict management and peer mediation programs in school.
- Substance abuse prevention programs including alcohol, tobacco, inhalants and other drugs.
- School policy on threats or threatening situations.
- Gang prevention program.
- School safety.
- Gun safety courses.
- Day-care and after-school care.
- Tutoring programs, sports league, clubs, and volunteer opportunities for children and youth.

What Can Communities Do?

Schools function within the broader community. Participation from families, communities, businesses, health and social agencies, police, juvenile authorities and civic organizations is necessary to successfully intervene and prevent school violence. Individually and collectively, community organizations have a great deal to contribute. They can share information with schools on:

- Youth crime.
- Systems for measuring the levels of violence.
- Sources of funding.
- Volunteers.
- Learning opportunities and materials.
- Services and programs for youth.

Using these resources and creating successful partnerships to reduce school violence requires strong leadership from school officials. After all, workable school-community partnership invites multiple perspectives and allows for the sharing of responsibilities and accomplishments.

School administrators and personnel, students, parents and community leaders have different perceptions of school crime. These different perceptions can sometimes make it difficult to agree on the primary school crime and safety issues that need to be addressed. Because perceptions of problems are not always accurate, it is important to know which problems are real, and act accordingly. In developing a comprehensive school violence prevention plan, communities and schools should seek consensus on the primary issues. This can only occur when people become informed by examining information from several sources and sharing the information.

Once the effort to collect data has been established, it is important to establish a systematic means of tracking infractions by students, identifying problem areas, and examining trends. One might consider surveying to assess priorities and topics. Other techniques might include talking to focus groups and interviewing students and staff.

Set measurable goals and objectives. Goals and objectives are based on accurate data and the identification of school problems. Realistic and attainable goals lead to greater commitment and long-term success. Partners find that goals are more readily achieved when specific, manageable tasks are assigned to small groups of dedicated individuals.

Examples of Collaborators on School Crime Prevention

- Superintendents, school board members, principals, teachers, counselors, coaches, school nurses, security officers, students, peers.
- Community residents.
- Siblings.
- Parents.
- Law enforcement officers, probation officers, juvenile court counselors.
- Mayors, city council members, county commissioners, and other elected officials.
- Volunteers from parent-teacher associations.
- Community and professional agencies.

- Nonprofit organizations.
- Religious groups.
- State and federal agencies.
- Businesses.
- Teachers' Unions.
- Colleges and universities.
- Health and social services agencies.
- Media.
- Sports and recreation facilities, parks.
- Boys' and girls' clubs.
- Youth-serving organizations.
- Chambers of commerce.

Sources of Data for Assessing School Crime

- School incident reports.
- Juvenile arrests.
- Juvenile court case dispositions.
- Social services data.
- School injury and hospital data.
- Mental health services.
- Student interviews, focus groups and observations.

Examples of Goals and Objectives

Goal: Decrease weapons on school campus.

Objective 1: School officials will enforce the no weapons on school grounds state mandate.

Objective 2: Conduct a media campaign for student, parent and community awareness of weapons being illegal.

Objective 3: School resource officer will train faculty and staff on detecting weapons.

Objective 4: Raise money to purchase hand-held metal detectors.

Objective 5: Evaluate progress and compare number of incidents to that in last year's report.

Appropriate Research-Based Programs

Although some programs and strategies are more effective than others, there is no single program or strategy to meet the needs of all students. The best approach is a combination of programs and strategies based on the goals, objectives, needs and resources identified in the comprehensive plan. The plan should offer some programs and strategies to the entire student body and direct others toward at-risk students.

When selecting programs and strategies, consider the following:

- Evidence of past effectiveness.
- The match between the program or strategy and the comprehensive violence prevention plan's goals and objectives.
- The reading level of educational materials included in the program.
- The appropriateness of cultural images used by the program.

Implement the Plan

Communities will differ in the way they implement their comprehensive plans. Certain steps should be generic to all. The steps may include:

Phase I: Getting Ready

- Obtain district approvals.
- Seek community support through a public awareness campaign.
- Train staff.
- Select students for participation in programs.
- Seek parental approval for student participation in programs.

School district officials may have to approve the selection of programs as well as any evaluation instruments. A broad campaign in the local community is appropriate for some program interventions, raising awareness of the school violence problem, introducing the intervention, explaining the process, and inviting expertise, volunteers, and donations. In addition, staff development enhances the consistency and quality of program delivery and builds enthusiasm for the program.

Phase II: Implementation

Continuous monitoring and assessment are critical steps in implementing the plan. The following questions should be asked:

- Have procedures been developed for monitoring the implementation of the plan?
- Is there consistency between the plan and actual events?
- Do budgeted costs match actual costs?
- What is the initial response of students, staff and parents to the plan?
- Are there barriers to implementation?
- What are the negative consequences of selected programs or strategies?
- What changes in the nature of the problem have evolved over time?
- What adjustments need to be made in the plan?

Evaluate the Plan

Evaluation is a critical component of any school violence prevention plan. It serves several purposes:

- To increase the effectiveness of management and administration of the plan.
- To document that objectives have been met.
- To determine the overall effectiveness of the plan, its programs, and strategies.

Revise the Plan on the Basis of the Evaluation

A well-designed plan will produce useful information. The results may suggest that several changes or modifications need to occur. Recommendations for improvement are identified through interviews with the stakeholders, surveys or focus groups. These assessments reveal which activities were most effective, what materials worked best, how barriers were overcome, and what type of students received the most or least benefit and why.

Everyone Must Take Responsibility for the Communities Where Our Youth Are Raised

In North Carolina, the Governor's Task Force for Youth Violence and School Safety Committee recommends that everyone must be involved in efforts directed at reducing youth violence and making our schools safer. The task force strongly encourages each of us to get to know our neighbors, especially youth, and to take action when warranted to create the type of society which will allow youth to grow and develop successfully. Other recommendations include:

- Current laws are directly related to young people and guns need to be stringently enforced. Thorough analysis of the need for additional laws regarding parental responsibility, access to and the transfer or sale of guns, must be conducted. Continued efforts to promote gun safety education are encouraged. The task force was split between those advocating greater enforcement of existing laws and those advocating even tougher laws.
- There was majority support for parents monitoring video games, Internet use, television viewing, music and movies.
- Consistent implementation of zero tolerance for guns, weapons, violence, drugs and alcohol for youth should be supported through initiatives, public awareness efforts, treatment programs, and offender punishment programs.
- There should be greater involvement in our schools and in the lives of young people by the business community, civic organizations and nonprofit organizations, senior citizens and retirees, and the faith community.
- Develop an aggressive and ongoing statewide public awareness which promotes efforts to reduce violence in our schools and among our young people—including summits where parents, students, teachers, administrators, and others get together to share information about our best practices and common areas of concern.

Law Enforcement Agencies

The most important collaborative relationship for addressing school violence is between the school and the local law enforcement agencies. These two agencies can assist each other by sharing information on the frequency and proportion of crime in schools in relation to the same types of crime committed in the community; by jointly defining offenses and deciding which acts should be addressed cooperatively; by jointly reviewing policies and procedures for handling students who commit crimes in schools, including guidelines for police entering a school, interviewing students and staff, and making an arrest on school grounds; and by jointly participating in planning and implementing programs to prevent school crime and student misbehavior.

Other items on which schools and law enforcement can work together include:

- Developing a school crisis plan.
- Developing a safe schools plan.
- Hiring school resource officers.
- Creating crime prevention programs to be offered to the community.
- Developing prevention and intervention programs on drugs, alcohol, violence, gangs and others.

Recommendations for Policy Makers

On the whole, districts which are working together to reduce violence are doing a good job. Schools are usually safer than the neighborhoods around them. The simple reality is that school authorities can never completely protect students or assure their safety from random acts of violence. There is a need to give emphasis and attention to safety issues on a regular basis. Three elements should characterize all safety programs. The elements include:

1. All stakeholders (students, parents, teachers, administrators and community members) should have a role in planning and implementing safety programs.

2. There must be a consistency between policies, programs and rules and in the enforcement of discipline.

3. Rules should be applied with judgment so that common sense prevails over mechanical application of discipline.

Recommendations for School Boards

The school board plays three distinct roles: 1. the formulation of comprehensive policy direction for the district; 2. monitoring the implementation and effectiveness of the district's policies, procedures and programs; and 3. focusing community attention on the issues.

Most school districts have multiple policies dealing with individual elements of school safety. Discipline codes, disaster management plans, weapons prohibitions, procedures for handling bomb threats— all of these are found in administrative guideline handbooks. However, few districts have comprehensive policies that make safety one of the highest priorities of the district.

The important elements of a comprehensive policy on school safety are:

1. A clear vision for school safety giving it high priority in a district's strategic plan.

2. The requirement for a districtwide safe schools plan.

3. The requirement for each school building to have a safe schools plan.

4. The identification of the kind of data that is to be collected to monitor the policy.

5. A commitment by the board to review the safety program on a regular basis.

6. A proactive means for engaging the community on matters of safety in the schools.

Monitoring for Safety

The board of education needs to monitor for safety because such monitoring forces the board to focus attention on safety issues and to distinguish procedures and programs that actually work from those that are not effective. To monitor its strategic policy on school safety effectively, a board of education must identify at the outset the kind of information that is to be collected and reported to the staff. Also, it must demonstrate a high priority for safety by committing its own meeting time and using its power to emphasize the importance of the topic.

Collecting data can be costly and time consuming. Therefore, only the data that will be useful in monitoring progress toward the goals should be called for. Several states are required to submit an annual report on school violence. The report includes details of specific incidents: incident site, offenders, victims, consequences and the number of student related arrests. In one school the troublesome problem might be weapons while another school might have a problem with fights. However, the important point is that the board of education knows the school sites and also what specific problems the schools are having. One school system in North Carolina gives a monthly report at the board of education meeting on the number of threats or threatening incidents which occurred in the system. This assists in keeping the board current and abreast of violent situations in the school system.

Emerging Safety Programs Common to Many Districts

For years school districts have been required by law to prepare and distribute student handbooks which include the student codes of conduct and the processes used to enforce them. How these rules are published and distributed can make a significant difference in their effectiveness. For example, in some school districts the rules are printed on wallet sized cards and distributed to all students. Another common practice is the use of agenda books; these spiral student handbooks contain rules and consequences and other items such as school calendar, athletic schedule, important dates to remember, helpful suggestions for reading, and even the metric system of weights and measures.

Other common practices emerging to enforce and supplement school rules include:

- Safety Committees. Districts are creating various safety committees. Sometimes composed of students within schools and often made up of adults and students from different districts, their function is: (1) to identify problems and concerns; (2) to suggest solutions and initiatives; (3) to keep a focus of attention on the importance of safety issues; and (4) to engage more than the district staff in assuming responsibility for safety issues.
- Security Personnel. Increasingly school districts are hiring in-school security staff. They may be uniformed police officers assigned to school full or part-time or they may be specially trained staff with the responsibility to patrol the school and work

with students and other staff to promote safety. Many larger districts have created the role of director of security and assigned that person the responsibility of developing and managing the district's safety program.

- School Resource Officers. A certified law enforcement officer who is permanently assigned to provide coverage to a school or a set of schools, the SRO is specifically trained to perform their roles: law enforcement officer; law-related counselor; and law-related education teacher. The SRO is not a security guard or officer who has been placed temporarily in a school in response to a crisis situation, but rather acts as a comprehensive resource for their school.
- Crisis Management Plans and Training. Many districts provide specific training to staff for managing crises such as suicide, death, intruders on campus, weapons possession and natural disasters, as well as preventive training relating to safety issues such as gang recognition, conflict resolution and harassment prevention.
- Personal Identification Badges. Some schools require staff and students to wear personal identification badges. This helps students and adults know one another, and it helps identify who belongs in the building and who does not. Visitors on campus are also required to check in at the office, and they receive visitors' badges. Requiring identification badges is an effective way to monitor for the presence of outsiders who may be dealing drugs, involved in gang activity, or pose a threat to student and staff safety.
- Police Partnerships. In many communities the police are eager to construct positive working relationships with youth by being in schools and establishing productive, personal relationships with students. Such partnerships also enable school and police officials to identify standard operating procedures for handling crises and crimes and to agree on school reporting and police response practices.
- Alternative Educational Programs. Both legal requirements and common sense dictate that when students are violent or seriously violate the rules, the best place for them is not on the street. A structured program and monitored environment is essential. Alternatives ranging from temporary time-out rooms and Saturday school to full-time assignment to a specially designed program for disruptive students are being implemented.

- Programs Designed to Meet Individual Needs. Differences in custom and culture, variations in historical experience, and demands on facilities are so great that each school must address matters in ways that are unique to it.
- Using Technology for Safety. Video monitors are being used at key points on school campus. They are both a means of collecting evidence of misbehavior and a deterrent to such behavior. Other technology is also being used. For communicating on a large campus, staff uses walkie-talkies. Cellular phones are provided for off-campus events. Metal detectors are being used in more and more schools.
- Zero Tolerance Policies. Zero tolerance policies are growing very popular in regard to not allowing weapons and drugs on school campuses. Such policies are effective when enforced consistently and equitably by all staff. However, their effectiveness is muted if they are used to remove students from the classroom and put out on the street. Several districts use their zero tolerance policies in conjunction with specially designated centers or locations to which offending students are assigned.
- Last Chance Contracts. These explicit agreements give misbehaving students a second chance but also spell out tough penalties when a student fails to live up to the terms of the contract.
- School Uniforms. Schools are experimenting with a variety of approaches to establishing and managing dress codes.
- "Communities That Care." Schools work with other youth and family service agencies to identify and address risk factors that contribute to youth violence and misbehavior.
- "Children's Summit." When this process was used, parents, staff, students and other community members were able to contribute to the district's strategic plan. Issues of student safety emerged as a high priority for the plan.
- Annual Surveys. Students and adults in each school are surveyed to find out how safe they feel. The results are then analyzed and used to improve school and district safety programs.
- "YWCA Week Without Violence." Schools and community organizations cooperate with the YWCA in sponsoring events designed to foster nonviolence and encourage individuals to take responsibility and action to reduce violence.
- Activities for Teens. Many districts have joined with other organizations in the community to provide evening and after-school

activities. School facilities are used for dances, sports and other social activities. Opportunities to participate in after-school hobbies and extracurricular learning are also offered, particularly for younger students who would otherwise be at home in the afternoon without adult supervision.

- Truancy Centers. One large district has joined with the city to establish a truancy center. A student who is off campus during the school hours is taken to the center by police. The next day the student, their parents and the principal meet to develop a plan to deal with that student's truancy.
- Trespass Agreement. Districts have developed trespass agreements with owners of property adjacent to high schools. Districts have the authority to monitor the outside ground of those properties and to ask intruders there to vacate the premises; they can call the authorities if need be.

Working Together

Responsibility for curbing violence among children rests with everyone: parents, schools, students, the community and society at large. Diminishing the influence of media violence on children will require more than just parents turning off the television in their homes, or limiting what their children watch; it will require television and movie companies deciding to produce less violent fare for children and adults. Schools must provide services that meet all needs of all children. Health, psychological, special education, and other services have to be available in the school buildings so children can get the help they need. Police, churches, youth centers, park districts—all can play a part in helping to address the problem of violent children. Otherwise—as with any problem that goes unattended—the problem of violence and children will only get worse.

Violence in the schools has never merited more concern than it does now. Although some types of school crime have decreased in recent years, violence seems to be spreading and intensifying—not only in the schools, but also in our communities large and small. Educators, criminologists and law enforcement personnel have worked to create effective methods to control current school violence and to prevent such violence in the future. However, that's not enough. Until schools, parents, students and the community work together, this societal problem is not going to disappear.

Much school violence has its source in the community. However, intruders who commit violence were once students themselves; schools had a hand in creating these violent adults.

In a longitudinal study spanning 22 years, Leonard D. Eron and L. Rowell Heusmann of the University of Chicago found a striking stability in violent behavior over time. Aggressive, bullying behavior at age eight was strongly correlated with violent and criminal behavior in adulthood (Greenbaum and others).

By the time they were 30, the individuals in the study were much more likely to have been convicted of crimes; to have been convicted of more serious crimes; to have more moving traffic violations; to have more convictions for drunken driving; to be more abusive toward spouses; to have more aggressive children; and not to have achieved well educationally, professionally and socially. The results were independent of intelligence and social class as measured at age eight (Greenbaum and others).

The prevention and intervention programs described throughout the book are made up of proven practices—practices that have been proved successful in dealing with children with violent tendencies. If the programs produce the effects they promise, schools will have played an invaluable role in breaking the tragic cycle of violence. Helping children replace violent behaviors with effective, positive social skills may reduce violence not only in the schools, but also in society as a whole.

References

American Psychology Association Commission on Violence and Youth. 1993. *www. uncg.edu/ericcass/violence/docs/violence.html.*

The American Teacher. "Factors Contributing to School Violence." 1993. Web site: *http://eric-web.tc./columbia.edu/monographs/uds107/preventing-facbs.html.*

Bouyea, Bob. 1998. *Violence Prevention and Planning.* Horsham, Pennsylvania: LRP Publications.

Butterfield, George E., and Brenda Turner, Editors. "Weapons in Schools." NSSC Resource Paper. Malibu, California: National School Safety Center, 1989. 43 pages. ED 310 536.

California Department of Public Education. "School Crime in California for the 1988-89 School Year. March 1990. 33 pages. ED 320 225.

California State Department of Public Instruction, School Climate and Student Support Services Unit; California Office of the Attorney General, Crime Prevention Center. "Safe Schools: A Planning Guide to Action." Sacramento, 1989. 122 pages. ED 313 815.

Clinton, Hillary Rodham. *It Takes a Village.* 1996. *www.hillary2000.org/.*

Garrett, Anne G. 1999. *What Do American Schools Need?* Commack, New York: Kroshka Books.

Gathercoach, Paul. 1988. *www.midtod.com/bestof/children.html.*

Gaustad, John. 1991. *Schools Respond to Gangs and Violence.* Eugene, Oregon: Oregon School Study Council.

Governor's Task Force Youth Violence and School Safety. August 1999. North Carolina: Department of Public Instruction.

Greenbaum, Stuart, and others. "Set Straight on Bullies." Malibu, California: National School Safety Center. September 1989. 89 pages. ED 312 744. *http://www.whitehouse.gov/VVH/New?199904212176.html.*

Harper, Suzanne. "School Crisis Prevention and Response." NSSC Resource

143

Paper. Malibu, California: National School Safety Center. September 1989. 24 pages. Ed 311 600.

Kids Killing Kids: 1988. *http://www.familyvalues.nu/article2.htm.*

Linquanti, Robert and BethAnn Berliner. 1994. *Rebuilding Schools as Safe Havens: A Typology for Selecting and Integrating Violence Prevention Strategies.* Portland, Oregon: Western Regional Center for Drug-Free Schools and Communities.

McNair, Raymond F. "Teen Violence." *Time* magazine. April 6, 1998. *www. worldahead.org/wam/9807/w9807fl.html.*

Making Schools Safe. Western Regional Center for Drug-Free Schools and Communities. Portland, Oregon: Northwest Regional Educational Laboratory, 1994.

Metropolican Life Survey of the American Teacher. 1997. *www.metlife. com/Companyinfo/Community/Found/Docsed.html.*

National Association for the Education of Young Children. "NAEYC Position Paper Statement on Media Violence in Children's Lives." *Young Children.* 1990. 45(5), 18–21 (ej415 397).

New York Times. January 1997. *http://www.nytimes.com/library/review.*

Office for Substance Abuse Prevention and Public Health Services, U.S. Department of Health and Human Services. *Preventing Chaos in Times of Crisis.* Sacramento, California: Association of California School Administrators, 1995.

Postman, Neil. 1982. *The Disappearance of Childhood.* New York: Delacorte Press.

Safe Schools: A Planning Guide For High Schools. 1995. Raleigh, North Carolina: Department of Public Instruction.

School Safety Resource Guide. 1998. Westlake Village, California: National School Safety Center.

Sempler, Martin. "Preventing Violence in Schools." *AASA Leadership News.* 1997. School Law Brief 69-99.

Severy, Lisa L. "Preventing Threats of Violence in Schools from Turning into a Tragedy." *School Law Review.* NSBA. Council of Lawyers, 1999.

Smith, Helen. 1999. *http://www.violentkids.com*

Spivak, Howard. "Violent Kids." 1996. *http://www.fcs.uga.edu/outreach/coopex/ hottopic/violentkids.html.*

Sullivan, Patricia. "Violent Kids, What's Really behind the Rash of Violence Committed in Schools?" *Our Children.* October 1998.

U.S. Department of Education and Justice. Annual Report on School Safety. 1998. Washington, D.C. Web site: *http://ncjrs.org/jjvict.htm.*

U.S. Department of Education, National Center for Education Statistics. *Violence and Discipline Problems in U.S. Public Schools: 1996-1997.*

U.S. Department of Health, Education and Welfare. *Violent Schools—Safe Schools: The Safe School Study Report to the Congress.* December 1977.

"U.S. Schools: Security by Metal Detector?" CNN News Network, Inc., December 2, 1997.

Violence in the Schools: How America's Schoolboards Are Safeguarding Your Children. Alexandria, Virginia, National School Boards Association, 1993.

Weapons in Schools. National School Safety Center. Malibu, California: Pepperdine University, 1993.

Why Are Kids Killing Kids? The Nutrition Mind Connection. 1996. *http://207. 48.132. 28/issue/157-8/157kids.htm.*

Index